CITIZENSHIP AFTER TRUMP

In *Citizenship After Trump*, political theorists Bradley S. Klein and Scott G. Nelson explore the meaning of community in the context of intense political polarization, the surge of far-right nationalism and deepening divisions during the coronavirus pandemic.

With both Trumpism and the ongoing coronavirus pandemic greatly testing American democracy, the authors examine the political, economic and cultural challenges that remain after the Trump Administration's exceedingly inept leadership response. They explore the promise and limits of democracy relative to long-standing traditions of American political thought. The book argues that all Americans should consider the claims of citizenship amidst the forces consolidating today around narrow conceptions of race, nation, ethnicity and religion—each of which imperils the institutions of democracy and strikes at the heart of the country's political culture. Chapters on the media, political economy, fascism and social democracy explore what Americans have gotten so wrong politically and consider what kind of vision can, in the years ahead, lead the country out of a truly dangerous impasse.

Citizenship After Trump is an invaluable and timely resource for self-critical analysis and will stimulate focused discussions about as yet unexplored regions of America's political history.

Bradley S. Klein is a freelance journalist and landscape architecture design consultant. He holds a PhD in political science from the University of Massachusetts and taught political theory and international relations for many years before pursuing an award-winning career in journalism. He has held research grants at the Free University of Berlin and the Australian National University and lectured and consulted across North America, Europe, Asia and Africa. He is the author of

Strategic Studies and World Order (1994) and numerous scholarly articles and book chapters on political and social theory and international relations. He is the author of nine books on golf course landscapes and thousands of articles on golf, sports and culture. His blog www.coronavirusdiaries.net covers everyday politics and culture in the pandemic era.

Scott G. Nelson is Associate Professor in the Department of Political Science at Virginia Tech, where he teaches political theory and political economy. He received his PhD from Arizona State University. He is the author of *Sovereignty and the Limits of the Liberal Imagination* (Routledge, 2010) and co-editor of the *Ashgate Research Companion to Modern Theory, Modern Power, World Politics: Critical Investigations* (Ashgate, 2016). He has published articles in journals such as *Philosophy and Social Criticism*, *International Relations Theory*, *New Political Science*, and *Polity*. He is currently completing a co-authored book (with Joel T. Shelton) entitled *The Political Economy of Statecraft*.

"This volume is a passionate and eloquent warning about the dangers of Trumpism and the governance failures that killed hundreds of thousands in the COVID pandemic. A must read for anyone who cares about the future of democracy and citizenship."

Simon Dalby, *Professor of Geography and Environmental Studies, Wilfrid Laurier University*

"Combining impassioned concern for democracy and the public good with careful scholarship and perceptive observation, Klein and Nelson implore us to think about where the United States might be headed in the wake of the mendacity and incompetence of the Trump Administration. In common with the traditions of the public intellectual, they put political theory to use to argue for the restoration of a progressive democratic common sense. With nuance and sensitivity to the indeterminacy of the political and the fragility of democratic political cultures, they combine analysis of the COVID pandemic, the Trump Administration, and the rise of right-wing media, with examination of the longer-term and deeper trends in the American polity that have distorted and impoverished the public world. They worry—as should all who care about democracy—about the future of democracy, but at the same time offer hope for revival of a vibrant democratic public culture. This is an important book that echoes the work of the best American public intellectuals."

Stephen Rosow, *Professor of Politics, State University of New York at Oswego*

CITIZENSHIP AFTER TRUMP

Democracy versus Authoritarianism in a Post-Pandemic Era

*Bradley S. Klein and
Scott G. Nelson*

NEW YORK AND LONDON

Cover image: Britta Knappmann / EyeEm

First published 2022
by Routledge
605 Third Avenue, New York, NY 10158

and by Routledge
4 Park Square, Milton Park, Abingdon, Oxon, OX14 4RN

Routledge is an imprint of the Taylor & Francis Group, an informa business

© 2022 Bradley S. Klein & Scott G. Nelson

The right of Bradley S. Klein & Scott G. Nelson to be identified as authors of this work has been asserted in accordance with sections 77 and 78 of the Copyright, Designs and Patents Act 1988.

All rights reserved. No part of this book may be reprinted or reproduced or utilised in any form or by any electronic, mechanical, or other means, now known or hereafter invented, including photocopying and recording, or in any information storage or retrieval system, without permission in writing from the publishers.

Trademark notice: Product or corporate names may be trademarks or registered trademarks, and are used only for identification and explanation without intent to infringe.

Library of Congress Cataloging-in-Publication Data
A catalog record for this title has been requested

ISBN: 978-1-032-21483-2 (hbk)
ISBN: 978-1-032-21482-5 (pbk)
ISBN: 978-1-003-26874-1 (ebk)

DOI: 10.4324/9781003268741

Typeset in Bembo
by Newgen Publishing UK

CONTENTS

Acknowledgments		*viii*
Preface		*xi*
	Introduction	1
1	Dynamics of the Current Impasse	14
2	Social Distancing as Civic Virtue	27
3	Media	40
4	The Elusiveness of Fascism	57
5	Social Democracy	70
6	Pandenomics	89
7	Beyond a Momentary Intervention	101
	Postscript	122
Index		*130*

ACKNOWLEDGMENTS

The late Richard K. Ashley of Arizona State University was an important source of inspiration for this project. His priorities as an academic, and later as a friend, provoked us early on to formulate the main arguments of the book and, in some respects, we had him in mind as an imagined reader. Illnesses that afflicted him late in life were a motivating factor for us both. We would like to thank Josie Ashley for helping us arrange our last visit to see him in Scottsdale, and for her—and Amalia Ashley's—graciousness as our hosts over a difficult weekend.

Also providing invaluable support as both scholars and colleagues were Timothy W. Luke and Edward Weisband of Virginia Tech, Stephen K. White of the University of Virginia, William E. Connolly of Johns Hopkins University, the late Ekkehart Krippendorff of the Free University of Berlin, Stephen J. Rosow of SUNY-Oswego, R.B.J. Walker of the University of Victoria, Simon Dalby of Wilfrid Laurier University, Ronald J. Deibert of the University of Toronto, Ahmed Samatar of Macalester College, Christine Sylvester of the University of Connecticut, Mark R. Weaver of the College of Wooster, Charles B. Hersch of Cleveland State University, Cynthia Weber of the University of Sussex and independent scholar and photojournalist David C. Campbell. Three anonymous reviewers provided comments on the penultimate draft. We thank all of these individuals for contributing in ways large and small to the discussion that follows. None is in the least responsible for whatever missteps we take in the book.

In recent years we have also benefitted greatly from a series of engagements and conversations with a wide variety of friends from many walks of life who encouraged us and who we tried to keep in mind as models for the audience we seek to engage.

A considerable number of these conversations took place during and after rounds of golf, for which we are grateful to John Ammerman, Derrick Bushman,

William Cosgrove, Michael Gallner, Steve Greif, Vaughn Halyard, John Helsel, Brad Isaacs, Stephen Katz, Brian Kerns, Jeffrey Kreafle, John Mooshie, Doc Nocella, Glen Rapoport, Eugene Routledge, Tom Schneider, Harry Spector, Jeffrey Sterling, Marvin Weishaus and Renee and Shawn Welch.

We are deeply grateful to Natalja Mortensen, Charlie Baker, and the entire editorial team at Routledge for their thoughtful and expeditious handling of the manuscript.

Brad Klein has greatly benefitted from participation in a book group that has met monthly now for 14 years, as well as from a more recent James Baldwin study group. Four years on the Bloomfield (Connecticut) Democratic Town Committee have been eye opening with respect to local governance, with particular regards to Jon Colman, Greg Davis, Lynette Easmon, Kevin Gough, Rickford Kirton, Tollie Miller and Mark Saunders for their help in negotiating citizenship at that level.

Cory-Ellen Gatrall, Brad's daughter (and mother to his twin grandchildren) has been an invaluable resource on the pandemic in her multiple guises as a nurse and scholar of nursing, a women's health activist and a COVID contact tracer. And, finally, to Jane Nadel-Klein, who as wife, scholar and ruthless editor has made everything possible.

Scott Nelson benefited from discussions with Larry Berlin, Ed Conn, George Davis, Jim Martin, Aislinn McCann, Diana and Raul Peredes, John Rowntree, Timothy Ruback, Joel T. Shelton, Saga Schoffner, Nevzat Soguk, Dave Starr, Yannis Stivachtis, Mustafa Tagma, Lane Toensmeier and the late James P. Young. Scott would also like to recognize the input of his students at Virginia Tech, especially those in Canton Ticino, Switzerland, with whom he studied from a European perspective many of the dynamics examined here. Steger Center colleagues Sara Steinert Borella and Caroline Skelley provided assistance in the final weeks as the manuscript was completed. During Scott's long absences, Beth Peery was, once again, loving and supportive on the home front, and for this he is most grateful.

PREFACE

The last few years have been a strange, deeply unsettling time to be a citizen in the United States. If we are not careful, the next several years could see the political situation deteriorate further, and the country's path out of political darkness made much harder.

This book was inspired by a concern to map out the ground under which democracy and its many provisions can become imperiled—and also how it might thrive. Our sense is that right now democracy and citizenship are still in grave danger and that there are powerful forces at work seeking to close off the expression of behaviors and sentiments crucial to a thriving political culture based on decency and mutual respect and determined to face future challenges with intelligence and care. We draw upon the recent experience of the pandemic as a moment of entry into an arena of political dislocation that reveals both the gravity of the current situation as well as the enduring power of the impetus for active citizenship. The presidency of Donald Trump and the terms of succession to the Biden Administration are crucial to the narrative that follows. But this is not a journalistic account of the differences of two presidencies. Nor is it a journal of the plague years that engulfed one of them and continue to affect all of us.

The basic premise underlying this book is that the United States has reached an inflection point relative to its governing institutions and, perhaps more importantly, to the arc of its political culture. In the coming years the stakes will only get higher as the country continues to defer a reckoning on critical political and economic questions. The threat of widespread civil unrest fomented by the far right will remain with us, and it will be compounded by new and unforeseen challenges that threaten to make governing even more difficult. Our aim is to issue a warning, to provide a sense of perspective, and to offer resources for those who similarly feel the need to effect progressive and lasting change. We write not only as scholars and critical observers, but as citizens concerned for the fate of democratic life in the United States.

In this book we draw upon longstanding debates in political theory and political history to measure where the country has been and where we are headed. In so doing we hope to inform about a rich and engaging literature, one we have taught in our classes and engaged in our research, and to which we often return for inspiration and deeper scrutiny of things amorphous and radically undetermined. If political theory finds its true legs in times of crisis, this will prove one of those moments that gives rise to much that future generations will use to inform their own considerations of problems old and new, yielding further insights to reformulate and build, we hope, a more humane, just and dignified society.

Of course, these days one cannot be so sure what the future will look like. Ever since people confronted the horrors of the Holocaust and the accompanying disasters of world war and fascism, we have been acutely aware that it is not entirely unrealistic to imagine a future marked by the possibility of societal collapse, one defined—to invoke Walter Benjamin's interpretation of Paul Klee's haunting 1920 painting, "Angelus Novus"—by the piling up of debris in the face of which we find ourselves increasingly powerless. That fear is precisely what animated two generations of European scholars from the interwar period through the Second World War—scholars who assessed many of the risks and challenges we examine here. We have taken inspiration from many of these thinkers, and we leverage some of them to inform our analysis of the cultural drivers of far-right politics in America today. We also recognize that the problems we confront at this moment could become even greater and the stakes much higher.

The awful specter of a truly unimaginable series of events reappeared as plausible during the nuclear age and motivated us in yet another way to address basic issues of peace, security and globalism. Anyone who takes seriously the latest forecasts of climate change—with warnings about the acceleration of temperature rise and the intensification of fires, droughts, floods and other natural disasters—can relate to the gravity of what is now an increasingly common situation afflicting all societies. Ecological crises are entwined with the rise of far-right extremism, and both broad developments must be seen in the context of a host of human security threats causing refugee flows and mass migrations of peoples from places as far flung as Central America and Southwest Asia to North Africa and Burma (Myanmar). New and fascinating studies are now concerned with such "anthropocenic" developments. Much of this scholarship has informed our thinking on the special governing challenges the United States and many other nations must face up to in the years ahead.

Our focus here is on the immediately political in a time when the lure of a culture rooted in deceit, mythmaking and violence continues to draw people in. As observers, and on occasion as activists, we remain shocked and astonished at recent events (Charlottesville, Lafayette Park and at the U.S. Capitol on January 6,

2021) and the growing prospects of very dark outcomes. Any number of deeply troubling scenarios serve as animating forces in the following chapters.

Certain abstract modes of scholarly engagement as practiced in our discipline—political science—would repudiate the affective dimensions of many looming threats and instead hide behind the guise of objective analysis, what amounts to a form of political disengagement. Suffice it to say that we come from a much different tradition of critical thought and analysis, one that sees validity in a charged, not dispassionate, motivated inquiry driven by a timely feeling of urgency.

The critical nature of this work is inseparable from another dimension that moves us. We are, after all, citizens, too. We take pride in exercising some basic functions of what might be best conceived of as an identity. It is easy to overlook the more everyday quality of those experiences that we are given to think might congeal—almost automatically—through the forging of political bonds grounded in trust. There is, or ought to be, a certain pride taken in the mundane tasks involved in citizenship—paying taxes, registering to vote, showing up on election day and standing in line to cast one's ballot; also speaking out, voicing agreement or disagreement, attending school board meetings, taking to the streets to show solidarity, writing opinion pieces for local papers, and so on. These days those tasks extend to areas that were previously deemed entirely private but have now acquired a quasi-public character given the acutely public nature of a highly transmissible virus. And so, wearing a mask, keeping one's distance from others and getting inoculated have become acts of citizenship as well. Along the way such daily practices of citizenship have become heavily politicized, drawn into a volatile and obscene partisanship that warps the original public health function of those acts, turning them into badges of courage or shame.

One need only attend a school committee or city council hearing to feel the emotional intensity whereby current issues—such as what teachers can impart in the classroom, or whether school superintendents can make mask wearing mandatory—are engulfed in anger, scorn and accusations of betrayal, even as manifestations of an encroaching tyranny. What does it mean when citizenship takes on these hyper-aggressive forms of populist reaction, ones aimed at the heart of the sanctity of the nation's founding (however troubled) as a union of differences, orientations, histories, experiences?

By no means are we Pollyannaish about all of this increased cultural volatility. In the long Western democratic tradition, there is a strong culture of protest that we think is healthy and needs to be encouraged. When people of color refuse any longer to take their racist treatment for granted and rise up to protest violent police action or discrimination in voting, housing, jobs or education, those are healthy and much-needed expressions of outrage and resistance. The fact that they elicit "white rage" in response becomes part of the pathology that needs to be revealed rather than be grounds for backing off. Essential to the practice of citizenship is its enhanced ethos in such times, a sense that such civil actions are central to a vibrant, thriving inclusive democracy. Staying reasonably well informed and voting do not cut it anymore. Indeed, just staying informed is harder than ever given the persistent distortions to our media culture that are packaged as news and commentary.

In the Introduction we discuss the meaning of these developments within the terms of our own intellectual trajectory—or, better, our journeys, in a way that integrates our personal experiences within the context of the larger intellectual traditions that underpin the analyses carried out in the book. Chapter 1 locates these concerns within the specific ambit of recent political history and in terms of the fundamental impasse of a national economy increasingly unable to deliver on the promise of the post–Second World War American consensus. Chapter 2 shows how this breakdown undermines adoption of basic public-health management amidst a global pandemic. In Chapter 3 we explore the mechanisms of media transmission whereby would-be authoritarian, anti-democratic and anti-science discourses are circulated and become legitimated.

Chapter 4 re-examines contemporary concerns about the precarious nature of democracy under the light provided by debates that took place in Europe in the 1930s and later about the nature and dynamics of fascism. Chapter 5 then takes those debates and shows their relevance to developing a plausible, anti-authoritarian politics for today in terms of social democracy. In Chapter 6 we explore the social costs of an ongoing pandemic and the price it continues to exact in terms of civic vitality. Chapter 7 focuses on what is at stake in a political culture that, as evidenced by the attempted January 6, 2021, insurrection, comes perilously close to abandoning the rule of law altogether—and how this can be resisted by adopting more stringent inculcations of practical citizenship. We close with a Postscript concerned with the stakes for the country, and for the world, if we do not heed these basic lessons.

Through each of the chapters we hope to provide readers with an understanding of what has happened, about what much of it means in terms of the predicaments of power that Americans have for too long ignored, and to give people a better grasp of what these predicaments mean politically.

Politics is concerned with the prospects of a *common* life, not about ensuring that each person must be left to his or her own devices, the collective be damned. The old bonds of community that served to link individuals together have loosened, while new ones are the subject of ridicule and derision, in large part *because* they are new. This situation does not bespeak courageousness or national greatness. Holding up a mirror to oneself can be a painful experience, but a willingness to see and understand is perhaps the most important thing separating a world looking backward from one oriented toward the future.

Bradley S. Klein
Scott G. Nelson
January 2022

INTRODUCTION

This is a book about personal and political relationships in treacherous times. It was born of a friendship that happened quite by accident, as most all friendships do. "Nothing is more precious than friends; therefore, lose no opportunity to make them," observed the Renaissance statesman Francesco Guicciardini (1992: 44). Friendships bear unexpected fruit. This one grew out of shared if incongruent pasts that came, by virtue of several stunning developments in the American polity, to comprise a meditation on politics. This friendship was ennobled by the twin concerns we share for the fate of democracy in America and our abiding interest in the health of the country's political culture. Both concerns demand what today has become a rarefied form of inquiry, what may be our only weapon against a political culture increasingly ensconced in depravity and contempt, enthralled by an emergent politics of wickedness and self-abnegation.

This book is a commentary on the meaning of community in the context of politics, about the claims of the past that weigh on the present and the responsibility we feel to explore them and, in theoretical terms, to give others resources for doing so. The term theoretical is used advisedly. We intend an exploratory inquiry that is provisional, but which underscores very real stakes that Americans have by and large failed to confront. Consistent with the meaning and purpose of a theoretical exploration, our analysis is animated by a desire to embark on a journey in which one tries to see and apprehend well, to take account of a disturbance, a difference, a discontinuity—some foreignness when one ventures into unknown territory. A theoretical journey is well underway before one sets pen to paper. But by committing to writing things down one builds toward an analysis that illuminates and informs about that which hitherto had no meaning.

For several years now scholars and journalists—and far too many self-anointed commentators—have pored over the puzzle of the rise of authoritarian politics in

DOI: 10.4324/9781003268741-1

the United States, questioning its sources and significance in the context of the relatively recent historical experience of democracy and the political and economic pressures now visited upon nations by global capitalism. A great number of contributing factors have been advanced, from mismanaged globalization and maldistributions of wealth to a broad range of divestments from public goods in a time of regressive taxation and deregulation to the neglect of rural America and almost fifty years of middle-class stagnation. Each one of these factors is related to a host of others in complex ways, compounding larger problems—not least of which is the enormous challenge of governance itself—and creating new and unforeseen developments in still other areas of political and economic life. Rising inequality, environmental despoliation, the climate crisis, public health disasters in struggling communities like Flint, Michigan, the abandonment of inner cities, persistent discrimination against people of color, police militarization and brutality, leadership vacuums and sclerotic political systems—all these are contributing factors, too. And, of course, the coronavirus pandemic.

The full scope of America's governing challenges was unimaginable just a few years ago. Not since the Vietnam War, and perhaps not since the Second World War, has the United States faced an ordeal of the coronavirus pandemic's magnitude, while a president tasked with leading an appropriate response abdicated almost all responsibility to address the impact of the disease on the country's public health. President Trump's failures were legion, and they were enormously costly in terms of loss of life, economic dislocation, and the erosion of trust in government. But Trump's governing failures were compounded by his and his party's continued efforts (even into 2022) to turn Americans against one another. The country now finds itself at an impasse that, at first glance, concerns a basic ideological contest. However, as the country approaches a fascist syndrome (Polanyi 2001), the predominant ideology of the Right is now all but politically unrecognizable, a contorted and enfeebled limb of a terminally ill political body. Diagnosing this condition means pulling off a feat of political rediscovery, and that requires an effort to reconstitute the Left in the context of a dangerous governing deadlock. Ideological impasse concerns much more than Left versus Right, but bears instead on the culmination of structural developments that were underway long before 2016, well before "pandemic politics" set in. These developments include corroded trust in public policy, a culture that incites abject disregard for one's fellow citizens, and the emergence of a vicious and envenomed politics of scorn, resentment and blame that has crippled the nation's governing institutions. The country has witnessed the sudden appearance of a demonic politics that now sees government power serving and truly sinister ends.

The disturbing political developments this book surveys, and the sources of anxiety and resentment it examines, served for the authors as reason for a dialogue that sought early on to push beyond the institutional dynamics of political polarization and deadlock, a dialogue seeking instead to traverse the cultural landscapes of American democracy and American political discourse. In late 2019 we were summoned to a hospice in Arizona to say goodbye to someone who had figured prominently in our pasts, the person who was largely responsible for bringing us together. During those days in Scottsdale, shared grief over a loved one's end-of-life struggles sparked a discussion that took a deliberate turn to consider America's democratic prospects at a parlous moment in the history of the country, if not the world. The blueprint for the book was drafted before coronavirus emerged as a global pandemic, a development that only further exposed hidden fractures in the country's political system. Compounding matters was a neoliberal ideology that has been shaped by global economic pressures and which has exploited America's flailing political institutions and a culture averse to adapting to change.

Our aim with this volume is to chart a course out of this current impasse. If recent social, political and economic developments—many of them long in the making—are to be reversed, and if the nation's politics can be placed on a sound footing in the foreseeable future, then the Biden Administration, Democratic Party leaders, and all aspiring Democratic candidates for elected office across the country must do more than seize existing ideological frameworks, adapting them to address urgent short-term and daunting long-term challenges. New frameworks of political thinking and action are now necessary. And in the aftermath of the insurrection of January 6, 2021, the challenges America faces are existential and more consequential than ever.

Perhaps more than at any time in recent (post–Second World War) history, the country stands in need not only of new ideological frameworks, but new governing cultures capable of anchoring ideological assumptions and values. Ideologies and cultures are curious things. They are slowly developing structures of power. They are also notoriously difficult to bend to a collective will. Yet, new strategies of collective organization must be fashioned to address the great number of perils the country now faces. They will demand deliberate, arduous and continuous work by leaders and ordinary citizens alike. These strategies must be geared not only toward elected office capture, but should also foster focused conversations across the political spectrum, especially among the young, about the mounting political stakes that ordinary people now face. These conversations will need to consider how the country wound up in such perilous circumstances and how democracy can be revitalized to serve the common good. The book's main objective is to make progress on these two fronts.

Over a decade ago a noble effort of this kind addressed many of the same problems we confront in 2022. The political philosopher Sheldon Wolin warned some years ago about the rise of the corporate seizure of politics and the dangers de-democratization posed to the country's political culture and institutions (Wolin 2017). Post-truth politics, dismissals of science, reckless foreign policies and willful incompetence were all endemic during the years of the George W. Bush presidency. The inklings of something far darker were there, too. The invasion of Iraq in the spring of 2003 signified dangerous new developments at home and overseas: an indefinite war on a foe as amorphous as terror itself, the Republican agenda of privatization and continued neglect of the public sector. Education and infrastructure would become two of the biggest casualties of the post-9/11 wars. The arduous fight for common-sense health reform in Barack Obama's first term suggested that stubborn structural (e.g., corporate-backed) forces also persisted. Under Trump, these forces proved strong enough to all but reverse what little progress was made during the eight years of the Obama presidency.

To be sure, Republican (though, strictly speaking, not conservative) ideas have been met head on with powerful critiques by a number of prominent scholars. Political theorist Wendy Brown and political economists—for example, Robert Reich, Paul Krugman, and Joseph Stiglitz—developed lines of analysis and argument similar to Wolin's, warning about left-wing complacency and a self-congratulatory attitude that was also evident during Obama's time in office, if not before. Other warnings have been issued, including Madeline Albright's recent book, *Fascism* (2018), Timothy Snyder's *The Road to Unfreedom* (2018) and Masha Gessen's *Surviving Autocracy* (2020). Major world newspapers and news weeklies (*The New Yorker, The Economist, The Atlantic*) provide a daily regimen of analysis and critique as well. The latter two have long been standard bearers of conservatism (and, more than occasionally, Republican ideology) and are now digging deep for a fundamental rethinking of neoliberalism and free-market capitalism. Notwithstanding all but universal excoriation, the Trump Administration and a devoted cadre of Republican supporters persisted, gaining traction even after the November 2020 election defeat, and as the costs to people's health security continued to mount.

We are acutely aware that we are not alone in signaling similar warnings about the enormous toll this has taken on American democracy. Yet, what is most striking is the paucity of political analysis devoted to the work of ideological *affirmation* in the face of the steady progression of anti-democratic forces. If others seek to account for some of the same predicaments we address in this book, most have side-stepped crucial aspects of the larger political and economic context relative to the failure of most Americans to consider what this context—stretching back at least as far as the Vietnam War—has meant politically. We issue a plea for reconsidering this context and its lasting political meaning long after the developments that were initiated appear to have run their course.

The journalist Fintan O'Toole recently observed that Americans suffer today from a specious political condition of "excessive history" (O'Toole 2020). History abounds—meaning that historical pronouncements come at us in great number and at warp speed. Yet, history is obliterated just as much as it is over-produced. We are presented with quantities of history that cannot possibly be consumed, let alone culled through with care. So many dispositions of what might be called "historical seizure" stand ready to fit Americans with straightjacketed conceptions of what the past shall be made to mean at *this* particular moment, given *these* imperatives and *that* enemy who stands poised to assault or in some way insult the nation's essential, time-honored character. Witness a presidential press spokesperson who in the final months of the Trump Administration compared Trump's deployment of troops in Lafayette Park in June of 2020 to Winston Churchill's wartime leadership (O'Toole 2020).

To a large degree, Americans have tired of trying to keep up as the nonsense and insanity of Trump and his Republican enablers only grew (indeed, continue to grow). Consequently, many lost focus or simply checked out. That has proven very costly.

What is the meaning today of the civil rights struggles of the 1960s? Of the Vietnam War? Of the "lost decade" of the 1970s? Of the election of Ronald Reagan and the crippling recession of 1981–1983, and the exuberant resurgence of the United States in the final years of the Cold War? Of the Iran-Contra scandal? Of the collapse of the Cold War system, and of the great geopolitical uncertainties that followed the implosion of the Soviet Union? What is the meaning today of the Great Recession, of the Mueller Report, of a president who was impeached twice but never convicted of his crimes, and who proceeded to incite an insurrectionary assault on the U.S. Capitol while his party drafted voter suppression laws throughout the country?

What is the meaning of the rise of China—an economy that was basically nonexistent in 1978 when Deng Xiaoping put the nation on a furious course to catch up with the West? What is the meaning of the United States' response to the attacks of September 11, two major wars in the Middle East, one of which—Afghanistan—finally came to a close as we finished this book, but which may be best remembered as the most protracted failed military mission in the country's history? What is the meaning of the Global War on Terror (GWOT)? What is the meaning of the election of Barack Obama in 2008, and what does Trump's election in 2016 mean coming after Obama's eight years in office? What is the legacy of the "Big Lie" that led to the attack on the Capitol Building and subsequent Republican obstructionism in Congress? Can the effort to bring the pandemic to heel provide a template for restoring faith in the capacity of government to address enormous problems that have consequences for everyone?

We pose these questions to highlight concerns that bear upon the significance of political memory for a country that prides itself on a no-holds-barred orientation toward the future—a country that, ironically, now finds itself inextricably caught up in some imagined, mythologized past of national greatness. This Janus-faced disposition toward time is one of the greatest paradoxes of American political culture.

This book is meant to offer resources for delving into the country's recent history by sifting through some of the more important volumes of historical and contemporary information churned out on a yearly basis. A theoretical analysis forces a forthright engagement with many of the above questions about political meaning, about the political complexities of the past that are resurfacing in the present, but which now take another form. Catastrophes like the Vietnam War and the economic problems that afflicted America in the 1970s are just two examples of transformative crises with which the country was once consumed, and which generated huge costs that were widely displaced and distributed far into the future. The political residue remains, but too few today are concerned to work through this history to better understand how it informs our efforts to negotiate contemporary predicaments. That is, few today are concerned with the specters of these pasts and their multiple dimensions—political cultural, psycho-social—and few have inquired into the political and social values that were created by the fact that most Americans never deliberately confronted these pasts honestly. Fewer still have exploited the theoretical lineages to which we turn in the chapters that follow, lineages that can offer perspective, the handmaiden of any mature democracy.

In the following chapters we acknowledge our debts to those thinkers who have developed similar lines of argument in much different times and places. Our aims, however, are retrospective as well as prospective—forcing a more sober consideration of the past as we explore ideas and examine dynamics behind a dark present and a fraught future. We are very far from the lure of "national greatness."

The coronavirus pandemic is considered in these pages as one of the greatest tests to American democracy, and perhaps the test the country has been most uniquely ill-prepared to face. We examine the pandemic and the exceedingly inept national leadership response for insight into what both mean politically, in terms of the promise of democracy and also in the context of several key aspects of American political culture. Our aim is to provide citizens with resources for self-critical analysis and to stimulate discussion of some unexplored domains of the nation's history that continue to inform inquiries about what has gone so wrong politically and what leverage points lie between the plausible and the possible in the years ahead.

A pandemic of coronavirus's magnitude represents a great number of reckonings now gripping the country. All of them bear on the matter of community and identity. We are mainly concerned with the prospects of democracy amidst the pandemic and in the context of failed disease-mitigation efforts. We are not principally concerned with leadership failures, which are clearly legion. In contrast, recent commentaries prioritized failed leadership over the political culture. Of course, the leadership failures have been there for all to see each and every day. Democracy's chances—and the cultural supports it requires—are much more difficult to approach. Moreover, we would stress that the presidency represents a great deal more than the man himself. Trump enjoyed a supporting cast of agents and a great structure of political deviance the likes of which the country has not seen, and which has still to reach its crescendo. The intensity of the vitriol and the speed with which people are induced to move from one enemy to another (this week trans bathroom rights, next week critical race theory) far surpasses anything seen before, even in the McCarthy era. It is astonishing to think that Trump has been aided and abetted by almost the entirety of the Republican Party establishment. In 2020, as summer gave way to fall, a political reckoning looked imminent. But things did not turn out as expected and, after the November election, democracy's prospects continued to be grim. What can be done to hasten an accounting of the damage and complicity in order to agitate for lasting political change?

The change we have in mind is examined relative to the unique pressures and incentives democracy presents to societies. Democracy combines two ancient Greek concepts—*demos* (people) and *kratia* (power). As a form of government, democracy is very old, but its ubiquity in practice is relatively recent. Across modernity few political theorists had very much that was good to say about it. Democracy represented one of the most unstable and unpredictable governing forms, always at risk of devolving into licentiousness. Long before governments dedicated serious resources to ensuring that a wide swath of the public had access to education, leading political thinkers expressed caution about the political provisions afforded by democracy. James Madison is among the most well-known critics of democracy; his dark view of a power exercised on the basis of broad enfranchisement was certainly shared by many Europeans of his era, among them the conservative Edmund Burke. Deep misgivings were also registered by Alexis de Tocqueville, a theorist who, in the mid-nineteenth century, examined political transformations on the threshold between the Old World and New World (Wolin 2003). To curb irrational democracy, Madison and other framers designed a number of institutional circuit breakers in America's political system, including the Electoral College, to protect the Constitution and the republic from assault by the "rabble"—the contentious revolt-prone elements of the general populous. Their worry was a bandit democracy.

America's experience with democracy has been mixed, to say the least. The Civil Rights Movement of the 1960s is still the highwater mark; darker periods, including those of the past five years, must give even the most ardent supporter pause. Pronouncements of "freedom, God, and country" bespeak a level of political intoxication that eclipses prevalent forms of religious devotion, especially when uttered in the midst of a public-health emergency. It truly astounds, but should not surprise, when self-appointed militias get involved, threatening citizens and lawmakers at state capitals and in Congress itself.

More than two hundred years ago, Edmund Burke worried about the fate of freedom-loving movements and issued a stern warning to the revolutionaries of 1789: "The effect of liberty to individuals is that they may do what they please; we ought to see what it will please them to do" (Burke 1987: 8).

Notwithstanding the Democrats' electoral wins in November 2020, American democracy now finds itself on life support. Surprisingly few people appear willing to consider what perils the country faces absent an institutional system of checks and balances and a free and vibrant press, much less what such a strong anti-democratic culture means in terms of the ideal of a self-governing people. What does it even mean for the people to hold power when they prove so adroit at cutting away at the thin fabric of community that sustains the basis for the nation itself?

We start from the premise that the election of Donald Trump in 2016 was not an accident, not the "black miracle" event that, save one or two missed opportunities by the Democratic Party, would never have happened. It was not (or not only) the sudden and catastrophic culmination of a series of recent missteps of contemporary party politics, principally Republican but in too many instances Democratic as well. Rather, Trump's presidency and his near re-election in 2020 mark the penultimate stage in a series of crises that have afflicted the American polity since the early 1960s, crises that lingered and festered, never being resolved, scarcely ever questioned, and soon to reemerge in new forms, spurring wholly unpredictable developments in entirely different times. We say penultimate because the current period of anti-democratic politics appears to be transitional (what period is not?). We wager it will lead to one of two outcomes, which we will consider momentarily and then in more detail later in the book. Our point is that underlying tensions in the American polity have delivered us to a very dangerous political moment. Trump's election shocked many, but it should have surprised no one.

As of this writing, no significant cracks in the Republican Party (other than a few ritualistic dissenting Tweets) have yet emerged. Trumpism appears emboldened and could certainly eke out more election wins in the years ahead. Evidence of his incompetence, ignorance and treachery continues to mount; his party's complicity in his mismanagement, and in his crimes (not least of which was his serial commitment to the obstruction of justice, colluding with foreign agents in the subversion of democratic elections, and releasing five thousand Afghan rebels to buy a few months of cease fire), deserve even greater condemnation. Even an overtly announced scheme to dismantle parts of the United States Postal Service in an effort to stall the delivery of mail-in ballots seems hardly to have aroused the ire, much less the opposition, of Republicans in Washington. Based on the votes in Trump's second impeachment trial, that support did not waiver.

Our objective, then, is to present an analysis that forces a consideration of past structures and dynamics and builds toward new ideological commitments and governing cultures that can aid an anemic and still too disorganized Left in the United States. While it is certainly not novel to say that the political times are bewildering, it is nonetheless important to account for the sudden cascade of social and political ills against the backdrop of America's recent political history, and in particular against developments in political culture and political economy. At the moment of writing the world remains in the grip of a pandemic that has shattered our sense of the known and familiar. As of early 2022 the sectors of the American economy most impacted by the coronavirus (health care, education) continue in freefall, and the search for enduring meaning to such widespread suffering is all but futile when the causes of the suffering continue to cascade, and a second round of rescue comes very late in the day. Too few hand holds are available to help us maintain our balance and adjust position, leading to a sickening, morally depleting feeling of precarity and fear. Careful probity of personal as well as national situations and circumstances seems an all-too-fleeting exercise as we race to track the next new developments, surveying the damage as we move from one news story to the next. Yet, resources for thinking about our predicament abound, and we want to show that we have a surfeit of excellent guides.

If the current period is transitional, what futures lie in front of us? We suggest there are two. The first is ominous and utterly dark, leading deeper into the abyss of political demonology and fascist-authoritarianism. The other future presents itself as an opportunity, the chance for beginning a process of democratic renewal. The latter future, though, requires a critical reconsideration of democratic culture in America. The reader will see that each of the chapters in this book is meant to build toward a choice that Americans must make between two emergent and radically different realities.

It is fitting that two voices are represented in this volume. A joint book on politics is something we have talked about for years, believing we had something important to say about citizenship that neither one of us could say alone. Lately, as the concerns that have animated our analysis reached a fever pitch, and as a feeling of urgency descended during the pandemic, we began discussions anew, directing our attention at setting a political agenda for a politically adroit liberalism in the context of the country's turbulent experiences with democracy and political economy since the 1960s. As will become apparent to the reader, the idea of political adroitness means, first of all, that Americans need to become more comfortable with ideological values that emphasize community and solidarity, equity and justice; all the more reason to do so in a time of such rapid socio-political and economic change. These values come squarely out of the democratic tradition, so we should not view them as averse to any quintessential American political identity. They can be put immediately to use. More than that, if we still wish to esteem the virtues of democracy, these values must be reaffirmed and citizen participation in a collective cause rekindled.

Shared grief also informs these discussions. A book that is a response to political anguish is related to personal and collective grief in that both ultimately derive from a regard for the other, for *another*, with whom one feels a bond. One talks to another about political ideas as a way to confide, to explore feelings of mutuality and also for the proverbial gut check. Personal loss sometimes provides the initial incitement to delve, as it did in our case. We have an imagined reader in mind who, like us, was rocked by the loss—tragic or not—of a loved one or a cherished friend. The loss of a bond causes a fracture. One may be given over to healing by recalling a story of a time in which the bond was sure, when trust and a feeling of unconditional regard obtained. Healing requires mourning what one has lost. Mourning is a labor, the philosopher Jacques Derrida reminds us—a work that is forever unfinished, cast into the future, courting oblivion (Derrida 2017).

Reflecting upon loss is very much a concern of political theory, an idiom of inquiry that we also share. Political theory provides resources for thinking about the past, about community, identity, culture—as well as about loss. And, of course, political theory is concerned with questions of power, especially its public nature and the ends that power is ultimately meant to serve.

Our chief concern here is American politics, but we explore a number of international dynamics relative to their impact upon America and especially America's economy. Though separated by almost a generation, we were both schooled as political theorists by some of the same scholars, many of whom were concerned with Europe's great political failures in the first half of the twentieth century. The intellectual antecedents and socio–economic origins of fascism and authoritarianism were foremost on the minds of many American post–Second World War political theorists with whom we studied, and whose great works we debated in seminars and in drinking establishments during college and graduate school. Hannah Arendt, Hans Morgenthau, Isaiah Berlin, Theodor Adorno, Max Horkheimer, Erich Fromm, Karl Polanyi, and Franz Neumann, among others, were refugees of Soviet Russia, Nazi Germany and elsewhere. Though we came of age politically in much different eras, our personal and educational backgrounds stimulated an enduring concern for the dangers of distant pasts and much different places than we experienced in postwar America. Europe's awful political experiments remained alive and very real for both of us.

As with many theorists who matriculated in the late postwar period, nationalism and fascism haunted our political imaginations as students of politics and culture. To witness their re-emergence in America confirmed our fears that these twin enemies of democracy and liberalism are not only enduring, but in fact are constitutive of liberal, democratic politics itself. In saying this we are not suggesting that fascism and authoritarianism bleed effortlessly out of liberalism and democracy. Instead, we want to remind Americans that governing forms (democracy being just one) change—often dramatically—over time. Aristotle, writing in *Politics,* understood very well the reality that no political system can ever be stable for very long and all systems inevitably morph into their opposites (monarchy into tyranny, democracy into anarchy, etc.). In an early–modern Europe, Niccolo Machiavelli warned of the dangers of many of the same political eventualities that Aristotle pointed out some two thousand years earlier. Neither theorist thought very highly of democracy, but both considered it important for government to involve large segments of any polity *if* the political circumstances permitted it. In unfavorable conditions, democracies tend not to be able to bear the weight of such social forces as propaganda and insidious incitements of racial, ethnic, class and religious division, much less outright domination and violence proffered by nationalist and fascist opportunists.

Though separated in time by a decade and a half, the present authors have shared enough commonality of interest and outlook, read many of the same historians, philosophers and analysts, engaged in many of the same academic debates, and were inspired by the same leading scholars in a great number of fields, finding common intellectual nourishment in each. Curiously, we each separately developed perspectives on the concerns this book considers; we did not link up until well into our careers. Not until 2008 did we meet and begin conversations that quickly ranged across the entirety of the concerns discussed here, endeavoring to answer a riddle about identity in relation to our particular career paths.

Each of us started off as academics, with expectations of pursuing what we understood to be a conventional career path, from initial employment out of graduate school to securing a tenure-track position at a college or university, culminating in a settled life among the professoriate. In its own way, this was a version of fulfilling the promise of American life in the post–Second World War era. And like so much else that formed the foundation of the American dream, the reality has been very different and more complicated than the promise.

Fifteen years into a formal academic career, Brad Klein decided for all sorts of reasons—personal, familial, professional—to put aside his teaching and scholarship and pursue what had been an avocational interest in sports in general and golf in particular. It became his new career path. There followed two decades of intensive journalism, though always with an eye to "getting back" in some ways to his interest in political theory. Scott Nelson, fourteen years Brad's junior, maintained an academic commitment professionally, one that included reading and engaging many of the same scholars that captivated Klein a generation earlier. He was raised on Brad's academic scholarship and later discovered his writing on sports. Thus was sealed a bond over both sports and politics that developed from a common familiarity with many of the same intellectuals from both the classical and contemporary canons. The result, over many emails, texts, letters and shared drafts of essays, is the kind of collaboration that brings to bear parallel if distinct points of view. These areas of vocational and intellectual orientation—one that is versed in traditional political theory and international security and yet committed to a language that is accessible, understandable and actionable—are what propels the book's narrative.

We live in an era when questions of public identity and interest can take multiple forms. That is in part the product of a rapidly changing economy in which old presumptions about upward mobility, steady career paths and advancement within a well-defined profession have become so radically destabilized. Industry, technology, education, and the country's media culture have all experienced massive transformations—and at increasingly rapid rates. And they will continue to do so. Indeed, one of the unanticipated consequences of the coronavirus outbreak has been to force a fundamental rethinking about the nature and organization of so much of our public lives. Space and culture of the business office, retail shopping and commerce, restaurants and classrooms, and healthcare facilities—all of these public spaces are now being reconceived in the context of threat and risk mitigation and management. Social and political life—and not least the obligations of citizenship—will need to be rethought in turn. The chapters that follow are an inquiry into a great many implications—political, economic, social, cultural.

We are both teachers as well as theorists, and it is heartening to record in this book our debts to some great teachers and traditions of thought that have influenced our thinking and informed this analysis. We have shared several who inspired us, and we are quite aware of their lasting impact on our lives; echoes of many are evident in the pages that follow. We try to frame contemporary predicaments of power through concepts—democracy, equality, security, community and so forth—that endure because they serve as gathering points for contemplation, reflection and analysis. These concepts are endlessly enduring, not only because they are essentially contested, but because people devoted their lives to their analysis; consequently, the labor of a political life is unceasing. In this sense we are mindful of the moral anguish that Henry Adams experienced, and which he registered in his masterful autobiographical *Education*: how to do no harm in teaching. Is that not the first question one faces when reflecting on the ethical weight of the craft? In another parlance, we would suggest that there is instruction, and there is teaching. The former proceeds by pronouncing, judging and condemning, and the latter by way of self-critical reflection, careful analysis and informed discussion with thoughtful, dedicated and hard-working interlocuters. The point, as Hannah Arendt memorably insisted, is to *think* what we are doing (Arendt 1958: 5).

One teacher from our pasts is deserving of especial honor. We are both deeply indebted to the pioneering scholarship and intellectual mentoring of International Relations theorist, Richard K. Ashley. Richard Ashley was a colleague and guiding force in Klein's post-graduate education; later on, he served as the lead advisor for Nelson in his doctoral studies. It was in conversation at Ashley's hospice bedside in December 2019 that plans for this book were sketched—a project to which Ashley gave his (somewhat reluctant) blessing, just weeks before he died. We dedicate the book to his memory.

Bibliography

Albright, M. (2018) *Fascism: A Warning*, New York: Harper.
Arendt, H. (1958) *The Human Condition*, Chicago: University of Chicago Press.
Burke, E. (1987) *Reflections on the Revolution in France*, edited by J.G.A. Pocock, Indianapolis: Hackett Publishing Company.
Derrida, J. (2017) *The Work of Mourning*, translated by Pascale-Anne Brault and Michael Naas, Chicago: University of Chicago Press.
Gessen, M. (2020) *Surviving Autocracy*, New York: Riverhead Books.
Guicciardini, F. (1992) *Maxims and Reflections (Ricordi)*, Philadelphia: University of Pennsylvania Press.
O'Toole, F. (2020) "Unpresidented," *New York Review of Books*, 23 July. www.nybooks.com/articles/2020/07/23/trump-unpresident-unredeemed-promise/
Polanyi, K. (2001) *The Great Transformation: The Political and Economic Origins of Our Time*, Boston: Beacon Press.

Snyder, T. (2018) *The Road to Unfreedom: Russia, Europe, America*, New York: Tim Duggan Books.
Wolin, S.S. (2003) *Tocqueville between Two Worlds: The Making of a Political and Theoretical* Life, Princeton: Princeton University Press.
Wolin, S.S. (2017) *Democracy, Inc.: Managed Democracy and the Specter of Inverted Totalitarianism*, Princeton: Princeton University Press.

1
DYNAMICS OF THE CURRENT IMPASSE

We are aware of the defining characteristics of the historical moment in which we live. There is no escaping embeddedness in the issues of our times, least of all when undertaking political analysis and prescription. To somehow rise above or push beyond and purport to analyze from an objective position outside of a unique space and time would mean reducing one's perspective to simplistic generalizations. Worse, it would imply that endeavoring to produce some kind of abstract, universalistic account is even feasible, never mind politically appropriate. Our own understanding of the way knowledge and values work is much more grounded, tied to particular moments in time. And while we seek to offer a position that does not get mired in the minutiae of the moment, we also think it is important to consider the emotional valence that defines the era in which we live.

There is a danger, of course, in being too near to something. All it takes is a bout of binging on round-the-clock-news or following the attendant commentary and postings on social media—Facebook, Twitter, Instagram and so on—to feel overwhelmed, lost in a blur of screaming headlines and events. That has especially been the case since the spring of 2020, when we started to outline key features of the nation's current political impasse, with the convergence of so many issues that present themselves as both tragic and terrifying.

Yet we also are motivated (and inspired) by the public response that accompanies these events—some of them, anyway. The sustained outpouring of protest at the police brutality that has destroyed so much of America's non-white, urban and poorer communities is a powerful assertion of public protest in the best democratic traditions. While there have been excesses, the overwhelming majority of the demonstrations under the banner of Black Lives Matter have been peaceful and respectful. One revealing sign of the way media coverage works in an era of relentless 24-hour "news" is that the various television networks effectively lost

DOI: 10.4324/9781003268741-2

interest in the drama of major protests precisely because of their non-violent nature. It was not exciting enough to garner the kinds of ratings producers were hoping for, so they turned the cameras off and it felt like the protests had just disappeared when in fact they simply became further ensconced in the everyday practices of a shifting political culture. News is about what erupts from the surface as anomalous. Too often, closely tracking "break-through news" becomes an impediment to understanding deeper, underlying currents at work in the nation's politics.

Yet there is evidence that the depth, intensity and geographical diversity of social justice protests stand in contrast to earlier waves of protest movements the two of us have experienced in our lifetimes. Both the Civil Rights Movement of the late 1950s and 1960s and the Anti-Vietnam War Movement that followed on its heels generated intense, sustained support and attention. Yet these movements also suffered in their impact because they became disconnected from larger social issues having to do with systemic poverty, colonialism and militarization. In many ways both of those movements can be understood in retrospect as precursors of the current protests. What looks promising is the way in which the latest generation of protests seems to build upon simmering discontent that has lately become joined in a more comprehensive discourse that questions the nature and limits of citizenship, power, equity and justice in America. The task for "episodic democracy," a concept Sheldon Wolin introduced some years ago to call attention to democracy's fugitive, all-too-fleeting character, is to cultivate bonds of trust and attachment across space and time, thereby preserving civic commitment and leveraging collective action to effect policy and institutional change (Wolin 2018).

It is hard to deny that the United States is currently emerging from a long succession of economic disappointments as well as abject failures. We are not referring simply to recurring, cyclical bouts of boom and bust, whether one is speaking about the 1973 OPEC oil crisis, the Savings and Loan Crisis of the 1980s and 1990s, the dot.com bubble burst of 2000 or the Great Recession of 2008–2009. It would be easy, once again, to get lost in the particularities of each recessionary phase rather than to see them as stages in the unfolding and deepening of increasing inequality in income distribution, the hollowing out of the middle class, the steady advance of poverty (especially in communities of color) and increasing economic despair for so many throughout the vast middle class. All of this has been going on, to be sure, and at the same time one notices the experiences of an ever-smaller elite cadre of businesspeople and celebrities who enjoy more wealth, more generous tax breaks and greater access to privatized healthcare and education. And perhaps most consequential in terms of the impact upon governance at the present moment (winter 2021–22) is how the Republican Party displays such ideologically vacuous opposition to the Democrats' post-Trump legislative agenda, addressing as it does long put-off neglect of the nation's infrastructure and proposing massive investments in education, health and elder care, and finally facing up to a host of challenges associated with climate change.

The operative concept regarding those who are closed out of the nation's narrowing socio-economic system is "precarity"—being in a state of anxious uncertainty concerning access to housing, healthcare and adequate employment, let alone never feeling reassured about long-term stability. This runs the gamut, from homeless veterans to Lyft and Uber drivers and an increasing class of freelancers in fields as diverse as manual labor, graphic design, journalism and teaching. It includes the range of occupations, from temporary faculty (who comprise a majority share of teaching time at many major universities) to migrant workers employed in agricultural fields and landscape trades. It also includes those employed "full-time" at sub-poverty hourly rates as clerks and suppliers in retail sectors. The pandemic has certainly exposed the precarious employment base of a wide swath of the American economy. But the bigger picture is coming into focus as well. Because of sustained attacks on unionization and the declining rate at which workers in this country are protected by organized contracts, it should not surprise anyone that so much attention has been focused on the vulnerability and exposure to viral infection of an entire class of employees whose "essential services" have heretofore largely gone unacknowledged.

Given the extremely uneven availability of basic healthcare in this country, and the high costs associated with private insurance, we recognize the ironies of an economy that has been exposed as one in which the lowest-paid sector provided essential delivery and transport services to the sequestered middle and upper classes. And it was precisely those precarious classes that were deemed "essential" and who were "forced" early on in the pandemic to choose between continued work (and exposure to the coronavirus) or the relative safety of homestay and with it, financial ruin. One revealing statistic about the extensive nature of socio-economic precarity is how few Americans have emergency savings of even a very modest amount. Data suggest that 40 percent of Americans do not have access to $400 cash in the event of the most basic crisis—home emergency, car repair or urgent medical need.

Traditionally, industrial democratic societies have based their legitimacy on the promise of a better life. The toils and sacrifices of each generation were supposed to be justified through the assurance, or at least the realistic expectation, that successor generations would have it better off and that avenues of advancement through education would provide a path to jobs that paid better, made better use of talent and created a modicum of stability and continuity. Without that promise, and without widespread belief in a political collective that was actually trying to make good on that promise over the long term, a society loses its moorings and becomes filled with uncertainty and despair.

The normal path for expressing discontentment has been the ballot box. It is surely no coincidence that a chief aim of the Civil Rights Movement was not only racial equity but guaranteed, unfettered access to voting rights. It took the U.S. Congress decades to codify those rights yet, in 2013, nearly five decades after enactment of the Voting Rights Act of 1965 the Supreme Court of the United

States voted 5–4 to void key parts of the act's oversight provisions, effectively leaving enforcement of those hard-won rights in the hands of the states. The result has been a series of restrictions on access, this time achieved not through outright disenfranchisement on racial grounds but through gerrymandering of districts, reducing the number of polling stations, removing names from registration lists and reducing eligibility for absentee balloting. The effect, largely undertaken by state houses and state governments run by Republican partisans, has been to deliberately target Democratic strongholds—cities, poor areas and those places with high numbers of people facing various legal liabilities—in short, the "precarious." In the aftermath of the fall 2020 elections—with all the (falsified) claims of "stolen elections"—some 20 Republican-controlled state houses have picked up on this trend and begun to implement various measures aimed at further suppressing access to the vote.

When voting rights groups countered in 2020 with lawsuits in the courts and various measures designed to ensure fair access to physical balloting through absentee and mail-in balloting registration, the Trump Administration responded with the utterly cynical strategy of blocking the U.S. mail through a managed work slow-down. This was undertaken in the name of managerial cutbacks but was clearly intended to throw the electoral process into chaos by preventing ballots from reaching election boards, slowing the vote count, and threatening the legitimacy of the entire election system. These efforts included obstructionist measures undertaken by Postmaster General Louis DeJoy, a Trump appointee—measures that Congress has failed to reverse because of the reluctance of Republicans in the House and Senate. This is how authoritarianism makes critical inroads: a basic institution of democracy that requires significant backing from career as well as elected officials finds itself in a considerably weakened state, unable to meet the needs of ordinary people.

The integrity of the voting process has become a battleground in its own right, something that played a role in the 2016 presidential election and was also at issue in the 2020 elections. There is every reason to believe that elections will be even more contested in 2022 and 2024—which is part of the reason why Georgia politician Stacey Abrams's efforts to secure voter registration and balloting have won her so much attention. The point to make here is that protests against police brutality have been joined by a movement that aims to foster widespread public outrage about voter disenfranchisement, political disempowerment, and a general lack of accountability of elected and appointed officials. Of late, bottom-up progress on these fronts in many states is encouraging. Still, the headwinds against which citizens are struggling—to ensure access to the vote, to fight egregiously partisan redistricting, to fund government, to plan for the future—remain substantial.

For all the talk about democratic norms and practices, the fact is that "rule of law" requires a culture that amounts to a fundamental democratic sensibility, one grounded in citizens' concern for the truth and a commitment to crafting public policy to meet massive challenges with intelligence and a concern for justice.

The law entails mutual sensitivity to compliance and cooperation, and a shared understanding of the importance of principles that transcend the immediately personal, financial or emotional interests of any one citizen or group of citizens. The nature of that mutual understanding forms a large part of the inquiry in the pages that follow. The point is that when those in positions of authority do not themselves adhere to those principles, there is a substantial risk of the democratic culture sliding into citizen and state violence. To a large degree, what is happening today at the state level in the United States looks increasingly like Russia under Putin—basically a gangster regime of privatized interests, selective enforcement, and an eagerness to rely upon force to "settle matters" in lieu of institutional safeguards and the absence of a commitment to amicable consensus building across value structures. In such a situation the risk of actual authoritarianism only grows.

We would hope that Americans are learning that democratic norms are fragile. It is a mistake to simply assume that people occupying positions of power will play by the rules simply because procedures for accountability and checks on power are written into a constitution. Sometimes it is possible to tip the balance of favoritism in government to the point where, say, the Senate refuses to carry out its responsibilities to preserve and protect the Constitution, displaying more concern with enabling a lawless executive or ensuring a seat for the base on the Supreme Court. Or, that executive might have the backing of an attorney general, and with it the entire retinue of law enforcement such that allies can proceed to break the law with impunity. And should the military align in such a way as to become an enforcement mechanism against domestic uprisings, then the threat of overt authoritarianism—and the grounds for civil war—become real. When a masked troop of armed forces from the Department of Homeland Security marches into a city during a peaceful protest under the pretense of protecting federal property—despite a lack of authorization by mayor and governor—and persists despite the objection of elected local office holders, the country has reached a dangerous inflection point. Such paramilitary crackdowns in Portland, Oregon and Seattle need to be understood not as isolated cases of excess, but as trial balloons that test the limits of public tolerance and civic resistance.

Americans once believed that such incidents were purely hypothetical in this country. But if the last few years have shown anything, it is that the threat of a shift toward authoritarianism is a distinct possibility. In such a situation it behooves us all—as citizens, as parents and as teachers of political practice (e.g., citizenship), and just about anyone who cares deeply for the country's democratic ideals—to explain what is happening and work to cut a path for a counter-politics of resistance.

Do students of American history and politics really grasp what it means when constitutional norms fail to be properly anchored, or what the implications are when countries revert to state-issued violence in the form of fascism, National Socialism or any of the many variants the twentieth century has seen? Beyond the concentrated efforts of many citizens in Georgia and a few other states—particularly those agitating against voter disenfranchisement—there would seem few encouraging signs. Resignation and despair seem the more established sentiments. History is an important measure here. Once the initial slide into violence takes place it becomes very difficult to rescue the polity from within. Among the powerful lessons to be gleaned from many nations' experiences in the last century is that fascist regimes have not often succeeded in reforming themselves. Instead, to effect the regime's collapse they have required total defeat in war. Only after almost complete annihilation were those nations rebuilt into modern democratic societies, with firm rule-of-law procedures and (in some instances) with early-warning mechanisms designed to prevent a drift back into authoritarianism.

While the threat of a major regional or world war seems for many to be an unlikely scenario at this moment, we are deeply concerned about evidence of increased tensions among nation-states and the failure of leading countries to engage in cooperative international relations through alliances and treaties, both old and new. We are certainly witnessing a shift toward insularity, protectionism and a "go-it-alone" approach, whether in the form of America's retreat from arms control, trade agreements or cooperation on international public health and global climate policy measures. Evidence here is all too abundant, including America's recent unilateral withdrawals from the Paris Climate Accords, the Iran Nuclear Deal, Strategic Arms Limitations Talks with Russia and, most recently, efforts to abide by rulings of the World Health Organization.

Great Britain's Brexit decision is another example of this troubling trend, and it should remind us that America's experiences are not entirely unique. The risks posed by nativist and nationalist approaches to problems of regional and world trade and cooperation simply exacerbate the pressures on countries to provide for their citizenry, and they only further inflame domestic tensions that have been building for decades. Such tensions are compounded by growing ecological crises—whether in the form of global warming, accelerated species extinction, more turbulent weather patterns or resource conflicts, including those bearing on such basic resources as safe drinking water.

While such lines of argument may have a screed-like quality, the aim of this chapter is actually more sober, and more limited: to call out the fragile nature of democracy in the context of America's recent political experiences and in terms of the long-term build-up of social and cultural tensions. That call is based upon the strength that derives from a shared commitment to the norms and principles that were supposed to underpin the American political experiment. While there can be no doubt that this experiment is at the present moment at considerable risk of disintegration, there are grounds for hope that the norms being trampled can be used as the basis for mobilizing a powerful public response.

However, we are not optimistic. For several years now a significant number of journalists and scholars have pointed out structural features of authoritarianism in America and in many other countries, highlighting the sources of scorn, anger and humiliation and exploring their opposites in the form of building commonalities among citizens at many levels of governance. In this context the history of democracy needs to be seen in terms of the pressures visited upon many nations by global capitalism in the last half century. While many analysts share the concerns we register in the following chapters, Americans' political attitudes continue to drift to the right and public policy remains stuck in the past. The consequence is that the country's prospects grow dimmer by the year. Throwing a spotlight on the mounting stakes and challenging citizens and lawmakers to work assiduously against authoritarianism's rising tides require a unique kind of perspective, one in which a rough accounting is used to frame the likelihood of several scenarios obtaining in the years ahead.

It is hardly novel to say that developments in national and international politics are both bewildering and benumbing, and yet it is nonetheless important to consider the sudden cascade of social and political problems against the backdrop of American political history, and in particular in terms of developments in political culture and political economy that have brought us to our current political impasse. At the moment of writing—again, winter of 2021–22—the world has been in the grips of a pandemic that has upended most people's sense of the known and familiar. The search for enduring meaning and context in a time of such widespread death and suffering remains all but futile when the forces of this dramatic health security downdraft continue so relentlessly. There are so few sturdy banisters to grasp as we cope with the growing unsteadiness. The conditions that present themselves lead today to a sickening, morally depleting feeling of uncertainty coupled with fear about the toll the pandemic will take on the population and the nation's institutions for some time to come.

Among the most concerning developments are deep and sharply divisive aspects of the structure of late industrial capitalism, aspects that are very much constitutive of the nation's politics today. Two prominent political economists— Jeffry Frieden and Dani Rodrik—have been signaling for some time the unfortunate reality that capitalism and democracy may not be altogether compatible (Frieden 2020; Rodrik 2012). To be sure, a purely predatory outcome has always hovered as a distinct possibility in this all-important sphere of national life—political economy. The attitudes of extractive industries in fossil fuels suggest this as one quite likely option, one which depends upon the virtual dismantling of the U.S. Environmental Protection Agency and the persistence of state and federal court resistance to what is likely to be a spate of lawsuits from ecology-minded interests and activist groups.

Indeed, there are not only strands of internal democratic resistance to blatantly exploitive social and land management practices; we also see those who understand the need for partial accommodation consistent with a democratic culture. Nothing happens on its own. The pressures behind an authoritarian slide continue to build and will require greater vigilance and political resolve to be overcome. It is far from clear whether built-in measures of resistance in the American political system will be able to fend off a commitment to lawlessness from within. Nor, to be fair, is it entirely certain to what degree those forces seeking to dismantle the government in the name of deregulation could achieve a concentration of power without the use of widespread violence. Fascism requires a level of coordination and competence that entails a fairly sophisticated political effort—acts of choreographing upheaval through violence at many levels. There may well be sources of resistance built into corporate America that will enable enlightened businesses to mitigate the worst predatory practices in the name of market share. Thus far, scarcely any business leaders have stepped forward. And to be sure, in such cases the fate of the republic would be in some kind of suspended paralysis between state lawlessness and the rule of the market—a stasis that would still not meet the needs of legitimacy for the vast majority of the American population but would, technically, fall short of outright authoritarianism. Indeed, the recent political deadlock experienced by Congress is best explained as a result of failures by the mainstream Democratic Party to appreciate the full scope of threats to the republic posed by Trump holdovers, not to mention a diehard Republican leadership that remains so skillful in creating opposition to even the most basic social and economic change. So very striking is the reality that some Democratic senators still holding office do not think democracy is at risk and think the filibuster remains a tool of bipartisanship.

The difficulty here in apprehending the full scope of challenges facing democratic prospects in America is most apparent in the altered *world* condition in which the country now finds itself. Unless we situate America's recent experiences in this larger context it will be nigh impossible to understand how fleeting are America's democratic aspirations in the years ahead. Important to consider here is the time horizon, one much longer than we are typically accustomed in a time of political acceleration and a fixation upon national concerns. It seems almost quaint to ask, for instance, what has been the political legacy of the Vietnam War and the 1973 OPEC oil embargo in the context of existential questions of America's role in the world (in the first instance) and the beginning of a long period of middle-class stagnation (in the second)? It is hard to make sense of these two developments outside of a broad, *global* understanding of decolonization and postimperial resistance movements. Such a framing is inconsistent with America's self-image as a harbinger of democratic universalism. Such a view is incredibly myopic and self-serving, as if the country were not susceptible to developments beyond its immediate sphere of control. Americans must reckon with the possibility that a democratic culture based solely on international hegemony cannot last indefinitely, certainly not without sustaining the realistic promise of its guiding democratic ethos.

Rather, it seems as if the moment of reckoning is continually deferred and, in the process, celebrated as yet another triumph rather than as a moment of recognition in which people take seriously the possibility of a defining national crisis.

There was more of a triumph than a sober moment of reckoning in the election of Ronald Reagan as president in 1980; something akin to recovery from the "malaise" of realistic reassessment that the Carter Administration had attempted during the oil crisis of the late 1970s. The fact that Carter couched a potential "coming to terms" with the American Century in a moralizing frame rather than in structural, macro-economic or ecological terms says a lot about the timidity of mainstream liberalism in the face of fundamental challenges. And yet even Carter was savaged for his modest efforts.

Likewise, the response to the near-crippling recession of 1981–1983 was an exuberant resurgence of America in the final years of the Cold War. The fact that it coincided with the internal decay of the then Soviet Union allowed leading opinion makers from both political parties to take a satisfactory victory lap in the ideological crusade that had shaped the Cold War without requiring any self-reflection as to the basic integrity and sustainability of the American project. It was under this virtual glow of geopolitical triumph that a national security cabal within the Reagan Administration subverted Congress and the law in seeking to channel arms sales to Iran in violation of an arms embargo and used the funds to support the anti-government Nicaraguan Contras. What came to be known as the Iran-Contra Scandal of 1985–1987 was another one of those quiet attempts of Cold War–style machinations to thwart the law and circumvent public scrutiny in an effort to prop up paramilitary regimes. These were not innocent little spy capers but serious attempts to subvert democratic accountability and to sustain violent, reactionary forces abroad. Great powers and empires never do "change" well. That is especially the case when a major part of the effort is to deny that one ever had to act in an imperial manner.

The danger of that denial is important. It means that one never has to own up to the extent of one's real place in the world and how that place is related to broader conditions of political and social order. For the entirety of "the American Century," which actually lasted less than half a century, the predominant or hegemonic status of the United States resided in a unique set of conditions that linked steady, impressive internal growth and expansion of the American economy with the capacity of the world's markets to absorb American goods and American dollars, all while nations developed their own forms of governance and industrial economy. In many countries those models assumed more of a planned agenda from the state, whether as the social democracies of Scandinavia or the more mixed-market models of the welfare state adopted across Great Britain and Western Europe. East Asian countries developed their own models as well and would soon present the United States with even more serious economic pressures, and later on, in the case of China, with geopolitical ones.

The Cold War had at least this evident virtue: it provided a convenient, black-and-white narrative about good and evil in the world. We leave aside for the moment whether any of those claims were in some manner true or adequate to the complexity of the situation they purported to explain. In fact, the world was always more complex, nuanced and site-specific regionally and culturally than articulated in the dominant Cold War plot lines that became staples of Americans' daily political diet.

The dissolution of the USSR into its constituent republics in 1991 provided a powerful historical occasion to appreciate the complex structure of the world. For too many inside the world of international security, however, the collapse became grounds for celebrating "the end of history," in Francis Fukuyama's infamous (and profoundly misguided) analysis (Fukuyama 1991). Interestingly, this was little more than an internationalization of "the end of ideology" analysis that sociologist Daniel Bell had famously attributed to the emergence of the welfare state three decades earlier (Bell 2000). And just as Bell's centrist, bipartisan analysis failed to anticipate the impact of the Civil Rights Movement on the American polity, Fukuyama's failed to account for the volatility of emerging world and regional powers and the demands made by social movements upon national and global distributions of resources.

Traditional international security debates were organized around the notion of power: who had it, who could use it. The notion derived from European diplomacy and a discourse known as "the balance of power" whereby major state actors kept each other in check by forming and reforming alliances to make sure no single power became dominant. The calculus of power was always a very fuzzy one in this world, largely predicated upon assessments of military force and the extent to which industrial prowess could be brought to bear through civic mobilization of the workforce and the armaments industry. The advent of the nuclear age in 1945 significantly altered traditional understandings of power, threat and participation in the international community. What came to be known as "the nuclear revolution" highlighted, to a grotesquely disproportionate degree, the ways in which force could now be applied as an instrument of state policy—out of all reasonable relationship to a standard calculus of ends and means. The risk of nuclear proliferation also meant that countries with otherwise limited military and economic resources now had to be taken more seriously as relevant powers on the world stage. This ushered in a steady stream of debates, policy proposals and efforts at negotiating various means to stabilize if not reduce the enhanced vulnerability of the world's major countries; measures seeking partial arms control on arsenals, if not complete disarmament of certain classes of weapons, became commonplace. Unfortunately, they did not always succeed.

The emergence of armaments as an agenda item for international security was only one of a range of issues that have come to the fore in recent decades and bedeviled the United States. These stretch across multiple geopolitical spheres, from climate crisis and resource availability to market shares, credit availability and trade pacts, economic distribution and the rights of minority religious and ethnic communities. All of these—the stuff of everyday life and politics beyond the minutiae of legislative wrangling—bring to the fore a variety of issues regarding the ability of any country to sustain itself in a world order characterized by multiple challenges to the international system's stability.

In part, these issues present themselves conceptually as the material of theoretical debates in the academy regarding the constituent elements of human security. States formally defined by separate, internal sovereignty all share a common planetary fate. There is no avoiding this. Worse yet is falling back on a model of domestic homogeneity that assumes the ability of the regime to draw upon the resources it needs and to rely upon the legitimacy of the populace to support those efforts. Those days are over. In fact, they never did exist, except as a figment of a certain desiccated imagination that serves the interests of the major powers in the world.

That is because in equal part to the conceptual dimension, these issues are also empirical, or at least factual in that they occupy a certain material reality in the world and have a life history that is unavoidable. Clumsy or self-serving government leaders constantly find themselves bumping into reality in the form of events and developments they cannot control. Back in the 1970s it was oil supply shutdown from a trade association of supplier countries—OPEC, the Organization of the Petroleum Exporting Countries. Today, the threat comes from a completely different place, a biological one in the form of a silent, invisible, highly transmissive and virulent coronavirus.

With such a wide range of challenges out there, the scope, nature and extent of the issues are understandably debatable. We could think of it all as "essentially contestable." What is most revealing about skeptics who want to deny the entirety of such embedded problems, or who wish to play them down as exaggerated—whether it is climate change deniers or those who dismiss the coronavirus as tantamount to the flu—is that they exploit the essential contestability of an issue as good cause for dismissing it altogether. The fact that experts can disagree on the scale, trajectory and duration of a major issue does not constitute grounds for ignoring it as altogether irrelevant or inconsequential. Far from it.

Given the enormous challenges Americans now face, we think it appropriate to pose two questions: What does citizenship mean for Americans in the first quarter of the twenty-first century, and what should it mean? We are, after all, emerging from a battering of domestic trials and global challenges that pose fundamental questions relative to what it means to live responsibly in the country and in the world. Those questions are all the more important given the rise to prominence of other countries whose cultures and economies are so different than our own and yet whose internal workings help shape America's quite diverse political cultures. Also relevant are some catastrophic foreign policy failures—two wars in Iraq within the span of two decades and the collapse of efforts to establish democracy in that country, the second undertaken ostensibly to remove weapons of mass destruction (that we quickly learned did not even exist). These failures suggest a deeply misguided set of policies that did not only reflect poor judgment at the time. True, there was a complete misreading of the moment and of history, one that Americans have yet to work through in any critical way. The same could be said of the many failures associated with the war in Afghanistan. Yet instead of exploring the virtually impossible—indeed, delusional—task of attempting to constitute a new nation and build a new state in southwest Asia, we seem at the present moment (and for the foreseeable future) to be a country that prefers to play the "blame game" of who "lost" the country. Never entering the discussion is what these two great foreign policy disasters mean for American diplomacy, for America's leadership in the world, as well as for the fate of many armed service members. Many of them are still dealing with physical injuries and mental illnesses, not to mention inevitably facing the realization that these two massive and hugely costly undertakings did not produce stable democratic governments.

Of course, it is impossible to understand the Iraq debacle alone without delving into the meaning of the political atmosphere in the United States in the aftermath of the attacks of September 11, 2001. Those attacks led directly to two wars, one of which (Afghanistan) would hold the dubious distinction of being the longest war the United States has waged in its history. The 9/11 attacks did not need to lead to either war. Invading Iraq was unnecessary and deeply destabilizing for the region, and crushing Al Qaeda in Afghanistan should have been undertaken as a CIA-directed mission with allies and operatives who shared the same goal. The equanimity with which both wars became accepted as constitutive features of everyday life has included politicians and media personnel of virtually every political stripe sporting lapel buttons of the U.S. flag that assert their bearers' affinity for an abiding patriotism. Wearing these lapel pins constitutes not mere symbolic gestures but signs of a need to prove one's loyalty to a *particular* vision of America. Like national anthems preceding major league sporting events, these kind of gestures are evidence of an identity crisis that needs to be rendered problematic rather than quietly acquiesced to. The smallest gesture of dissent from this assumed consensus—such as athletes taking a knee before a game—becomes fraught with signs of suspicion and suffices to engender popular contempt and professional disbarment from the sport.

We raise these issues at this stage not for rhetorical impact purposes, but to highlight a number of concerns that bear upon the significance of political memory for a country that prides itself on an unforgiving orientation toward the future, and yet, quite ironically, now finds itself inextricably caught up in some imagined, mythical past. What is the meaning of this strange Janus-faced politics?

We would insist that two choices now confront Americans, one of which furnishes answers to this question. One choice leads to further narrow political mobilization, more militarization and potentially widespread violence coupled with a rapidly declining political culture at home that openly tolerates—if not marvels at the theatricality of—a corrupted, self-serving Republican Party given to exploiting the uncertainty of citizens through divisiveness, idolatry and jingoism—all in the name of further consolidating power. It does so while presiding over the continued erosion of the American republic, an erosion that is very much in evidence in the country's inner cities, throughout the nation's infrastructure, and across its stressed landscapes and ecology. It is evident, finally, in rural, small-town America, those worlds most closely aligned with what passes today for a conservative vision of the nation, one which, quite ironically, constitutes its most threatened embodiment.

The second choice—democratic renewal—is in so many respects the harder of the two. It will mean facing some difficult realities that few nations, and few civilizations, have confronted before. It will involve sober and very painful confrontations with our national past, and with a consideration of the limits that must be placed on both public and private power. The climate crisis and various associated ecological crises must also figure prominently in discussions about the country's political future.

Like so much else that presents itself these days, there is no ducking these matters, or making believe they do not exist. Americans have certainly demonstrated a capacity to turn away from a fight ahead that will be hard, but they just might be induced to consider a necessary and important struggle rooted in the country's collective past, one consistent with a political identity now quite remote, but worth rescuing and putting back into the service of an altogether different vision. This vision is one that will be more consistent with the best of the nation's promise—ensuring the conditions for more tolerant, more just, more humane and more civically oriented and vibrant lives.

Bibliography

Bell, D. (2000) *The End of Ideology: On the Exhaustion of Political Ideas in the Fifties*, Cambridge: Harvard University Press.

Frieden, J.A. (2020) *Global Capitalism: Its Fall and Rise in the Twentieth Century, and Its Stumbles in The Twenty-first*, New York: W.W. Norton.

Fukuyama, F. (1991) *The End of History and the Last Man*, New York: Free Press.

Rodrik, D. (2012) *The Globalization Paradox: Democracy and the Future of the World Economy*, New York: W.W. Norton.

Wolin, S.S. (2018) *Fugitive Democracy and Other Essays*, edited by N. Xenos, Princeton: Princeton University Press.

2
SOCIAL DISTANCING AS CIVIC VIRTUE

One of the great ironies of our present day is that the best way to embody public virtue is by committing to the discipline of privacy. That is another way of saying how important "social distance" has become in our pandemic era and, with it, masking. A similar dynamic obtains when it comes to vaccination.

This was captured perfectly in a *New York Times* article from July 2, 2020, titled: "For Fourth of July, Officials Say Celebrate Freedom by Staying Home." Even as a bare majority of the country's adult population would go on to complete the process of inoculation, the dilemma of social distancing does not go away because the vaccine, while effective, is not foolproof; even those who have been inoculated can get the virus and pass it on to someone else. The sensitivities involved here became even more volatile with the advent of the Delta and Omicron variants, which spread more rapidly than the original coronavirus and exposed the susceptibility of even the fully vaccinated to "breakthrough" infection.

Meanwhile, those who have not been inoculated bear an extra responsibility not to pass COVID-19 on to others. With compliance made voluntary, the expectation is that we should trust those who have decided not to get vaccinated that they will act responsibly and wear a mask. Given the underlying politics of those who opt not to get the vaccine, they are being asked to uphold a level of probity and civic virtue that can scarcely be defended.

It was not always this way. For example, the development of other vaccines against diphtheria, polio, rabies, tetanus, tuberculosis and whooping cough (pertussis) was greeted eagerly and with relief. They were widely adopted and are now standard. However, this is one of those occasions when an historically necessary development arises out of unique circumstances to reveal the underlying character of a society. No issue in recent times has more clearly revealed the tensions inherent in liberal, democratic society between public obligation and personal

DOI: 10.4324/9781003268741-3

responsibility. It might even be said that this became a life and death issue. That has been the case not only for those sectors of the population most immediately vulnerable to infection and catastrophic illness from contact with the coronavirus. The very measures needed to protect those fragile sectors of the population and to provide a measure of assurance to the citizenry at large entail levels of extreme discipline that have tested the tolerance of society to adopt prolonged self-disciplinary measures. At the same time there is good reason to believe that while the need for discipline among citizens has never been greater, the ability of the executive leadership in the Trump White House to showcase that responsibility and to "model" ideal behavior was never at a lower point than in the fall of 2020. It has been enough of a dynamic tension between the need and the capacity to create what might be called an acute political crisis. The measures needed to resolve the public health issues were those that seemed precisely to expose and define the weakness at the core of the identity of the Trump Administration. Adhering to those norms constituted a political strategy that had devastating consequences for public health moving forward.

Like any book about politics and public attitudes and behavior, the present one is rooted in a distinct time and place. That does not mean, however, that everything in these pages is intended to address and resolve issues of our day. This is less a study of policy than of attitudes towards policy and the proper place of individuals in the process of policy formulation. As basic as it might sound, we also have to explore what is meant by "an individual" and how that person constructs his or her identity with respect to others in society. Only by doing so can we properly explain what it means to engage as a citizen in the world and to understand the obligations of citizenship as a life-affirming activity rather than as some rote, administrative burden. That kind of identity can take multiple forms and comes to us filtered through distinct historical and theoretical traditions that continue to play out with profound consequences. Any understanding of citizenship and morality must at least draw upon those strands of thinking and practice—local and global, though primarily national—that long precede the immediate stream of news and issues that might trouble us at any given time.

It helps when framing an issue to understand that many of the dilemmas we face today are essentially revised or altered forms of problems that recur in human history—whether of obligation to the state, the accountability of rulers to the populace, the threat of a slide to authoritarianism or the promise and limits of popular rule. In this sense, thinking about these issues draws upon a well-defined lineage, one that invariably involves such carefully studied thinkers as Plato, Aristotle, Niccolo Machiavelli, Thomas Hobbes, John Locke and John Stuart Mill. Along the way, there is also a more critical tradition, one that is variously responding to these classical writers and situates its concerns in ways embedded in the contemporary issues of their—and our—times. This more critical tradition runs the gamut, from Karl Marx and Friedrich Nietzsche to iconoclasts like Thorstein Veblen, Walter Benjamin, Antonio Gramsci, Karl Polanyi and Hannah Arendt. The writings of this latter grouping concerning democratic political culture and markets were heavily influenced by looming threats of empire and/or authoritarianism. They were concerned to shore up democratic culture because they knew it was fragile and susceptible to breakdown. They also knew that understanding political culture and citizenship required a much deeper understanding of human reason and unreason, and that it required an immersion in motives that went far beyond the kind of "interest group" politics of utilitarian, benefit–cost calculus that had informed so much of liberal political theory.

Rather than argue this in the abstract or simply in overall terms, we have chosen to embed these more critical considerations within the specific developments surrounding the global outbreak of the coronavirus pandemic of 2020 and its continuation into 2021 and beyond. In this regard our inquiry shares many of the concerns expressed by recent analysts of authoritarianism writing in a popular vein—Anne Applebaum (2021), Masha Gessen (2020), Sarah Kendzior (2020), Timothy Snyder (2017), Jason Stanley (2020) and Steven Levitsky and Daniel Ziblatt (2019)—but embeds it within the specific dynamics of coronavirus politics.

So, the pandemic is our incitement to some difficult questions about the ability of American political culture to meet basic challenges. It must be acknowledged that, as it turns out, we do not have a good track record as a country when it comes to acting virtuously on behalf of the public good. With the country facing a double whammy, of sustained pandemic and the dissolution of our democratic culture, we would seem to be also losing ground when it comes to claiming, much less reclaiming, a commitment to civic virtue. This does not bode well for recuperating on either front. Yet it is exactly these kinds of cultural resources that are needed if we are to learn from the experience of fending off the anxiety of a sustained pandemic while reclaiming elements of a truly participatory political culture. We are taking a beating on both ends, and each side of the equation feeds into the erosion of the other.

We see evidence of this in small ways and in big ways. Early on in the pandemic, back in March 2020, when many states were initiating stay-at-home guidelines, and folks were only supposed to go outside for work, for basic needs or for light, unstructured recreation, there already was plenty of reason to be concerned about lax adherence to guidelines governing mask wearing: groups of people walking too closely to one another on paths in the woods; school kids yucking it up with one another in close contact, as if nothing had changed in terms of the need to keep some distance apart; families out shopping together in grocery stores instead of one person dispatched to buy for all of them.

There was a considerable sector of the population that conveyed a sense of there being no big deal to all of this; that the extent of a biomedical crisis was overstated, if not entirely manufactured; that the disease had been nothing but the flu, or that they were not susceptible given their age, race, income or sense of self-esteem. They registered their disavowal of the pandemic by walking about as if nothing was awry. No mask. Little if any social distancing. Getting "back to normal" as quickly as possible. They probably figured they were healthy. Many of them under 60 years of age also reasoned that because they were not in the most vulnerable age group they were therefore immune—the more so because they felt healthy and so could not imagine they might be secret carriers and thus potentially secret transmitters. Worse yet were those who dispensed with any reasoning at all and just wanted to go about their lives unfettered, free of rules and regulation or regard for anyone else.

What is so striking is the extent to which these sentiments of casual disregard, invulnerability and social indifference were operative, this time in the face of clear evidence that vaccinations are remarkably effective and that masking in close indoor quarters was a necessary suppressant measure of the aerosolized transmission of the virus.

If there were a Venn diagram of such behaviors it would probably show overlap with those who reject safety belts in cars, and helmets while on motorcycles. The difference is that those behaviors generally only endanger the driver or rider, whereas going around in public without a mask on, amidst a viral pandemic, throws everyone else into a heightened risk pool. It is a basic matter of respect and care for others. The same could be said for the decision to get inoculated—or not.

This disregard became central in the efforts at reopening our economy and everyday life. The emergence from enforced cocooning only functions smoothly when it is reasonably safe to be outside and next to others in stores, cafes, schools and offices. In the weeks and months after certain areas of the country allowed for initial stages of reopening, nobody had the slightest assurance that we were on the path to safety. The numbers of deaths and hospitalizations appeared at first to be generally down, but there were still plenty of hot spots that metastasized into major centers of heightened transmission. Even eight months into a nationwide inoculation effort in 2021, states were experiencing frightening threat levels as people who remained unvaccinated faced dramatically increased vulnerability. States with low vaccination rates showed acute hospitalization levels, with Florida, Mississippi, Louisiana, Texas and others facing such severe crises that ICU beds and basic hospital services for non-coronavirus patients became unavailable.

The tone had been set early on, when reluctance (or refusal) to mask suddenly became a powerful political statement. With roughly a one-week gap between infection and the appearance of symptoms, the whole country was flying in the dark without instruments and risking wider infection without taking such simple precautions as wearing masks.

Masking was obviously not a perfect preventive. But it was one of those proportional measures that was reasonably effective in reducing the risk of exposure. That is especially the case when combined with other basic measures, like washing hands assiduously several times a day and staying well away from people you do not live with.

The strangest argument of all against wearing a mask has come from those who think it looks effeminate. We all know people who think it is cool to be Alpha dominant. What is so interesting these days is the extent to which stereotyping ripples through the media world and comes back at us as a gendered identity politics. Candidates for national office sporting a mask are seen as defining themselves in some egregiously partisan way when all they were doing was trying to ride out a terribly unsettling epoch in hopes of getting back to normal safely.

There were other more revealing moments when the failure to wear a mask carried tremendous political weight. Some were aired on a daily basis: presidential news briefings in 2020, where senior staffers (and, presumably, knowledgeable experts in epidemiology) lined up shoulder-to-shoulder in a protean display of male bonding as if to demonstrate their invulnerability. This tended to weaken the message some of them were trying to convey. An observer came away with the conviction that it was actually part of the subliminal iconography—to show that the Trump Administration was not fully committed to halting the pandemic because it really did not at all believe there was a serious problem.

The evidence was already considerable in late 2019, with the White House having ignored early-warning briefings about a potential pandemic, to its dismantling of the high-level biological security team whose job was precisely to monitor such developments. The light-hearted dismissiveness toward the pandemic once it started to take root was accompanied by a refusal to take seriously the demands by governors in hard-hit states for adequate supplies of PPE—Personal Protective Equipment, including gloves, shoes, aprons, gowns, masks and eyewear. The President refused to use the emergency executive authority vested in the Defense Appropriations Act that would have enabled the federal government to mobilize for the rapid production of such emergency medical gear. Instead, it was left to the governors to rely upon meagre state reserves and to negotiate separately through private markets.

Moreover, the social message was made clear: an administration that did not seek to protect frontline healthcare workers directly handling seriously infected patients was not going to go out of its way to endorse casual mask wearing by citizens in everyday situations. The symbolism of a crisis evidenced by ubiquitous mask wearing would have been in sharp contrast with the message spread by economic advisors that things were under control, and the economy did not need to be shut down. Signaling a public emergency through adaptive behavior like mask wearing would weaken confidence in the economy and, with it, in the government that was handling it.

Beyond the imagery that would undercut notions of presumed invulnerability ("American Exceptionalism") was the widespread notion that asking people to stay home and keep their distance, to keep away from crowds and avoid direct contact with others, was a major sacrifice, or somehow evidence of personal weakness or a matter of giving in to irrational fears.

Evidence on a transnational or cross-cultural basis is notoriously unreliable in such matters. There does not appear to be any reasonably confirmed quantitative index measuring, on a country-by-country basis, actual social distancing or masking behavior. No doubt this will make for interesting and revealing future research in comparative public health and medical anthropology. All that can be said now is that there is good reason to conclude that compliance with mask wearing was lower in the United States than elsewhere, and that it came with more vitriolic expressions of resistance and outright protest than in other countries. It quickly became highly politicized here in the United States. No doubt initial spikes in infection rates gave way to reduced numbers much more quickly in other Group of Seven partner countries—Canada, France, Germany, Italy, Japan, the United Kingdom—than it did in the United States. The one Scandinavian outlier to extreme social precaution in the face of COVID-19 turned out to be Sweden, a country that relied upon voluntary caution among its citizenry but no requisite shutdown or mandates. Instead, Sweden banked its faith on the development of herd immunity, even though the experiment was undertaken before there were any scientific data demonstrating the extent to which those testing positive and either proving asymptomatic or who survived would carry extended immunity going forward. Not surprisingly, the result in Sweden—prior to the advent of inoculants—was a death rate four to five times higher than the death rate in neighboring Norway, Finland and Denmark.

Likewise, the extent of infection that ravaged the United States dwarfed the rate in such countries as China, South Korea, Australia and New Zealand. In all of those countries leaders modeled behavior at a national level in a way that took seriously the extent of the pandemic and the steps needed to reduce infection rates. Moreover, political leadership embodied that preventive—or reductive—behavior more consistently with a willingness to be seen in public wearing masks. The counter-model to the "go-it-alone" strategy embraced by Trump was the strict adherence to masking, graduated shut down, and contact tracing endorsed by German Chancellor Angela Merkel, who in her official duties took to wearing a mask as a matter of pride. It might well turn out that a PhD in quantum chemistry and a three-year stint in a research laboratory provided better training for meeting the environmental and political challenges of the twenty-first century than having sold real estate.

It would be tempting to chalk all of this up to the idiosyncratic leadership style of Donald Trump. His own personal vanity no doubt played a role in his refusal to don a mask. To an extent unprecedented in American history, a president's individual character traits became a basis for generating public policy outcomes. Of course, character has always mattered. Theodore Roosevelt harnessed a kind of manic *machismo* tied to a feverish oratorical and literary output that translated well into a policy of neocolonial imperial expansion both westward and outward. Richard Nixon's dark, brooding moodiness led him into conspiratorial scheming and ultimately to the treachery of Watergate and its coverup.

With Trump, the need for personal affirmation from an adoring audience, coupled with his characteristic indifferent regard for the suffering of ordinary people, suggests he does not consider all human beings as having equal worth.

Whether it is foreigners, Muslims, American minorities or women in general, he was unusually inured to their pleas for equity and fairness in policy and business. And then there is his penchant for storytelling, much of it seemingly made up on the spot in a kind of out-loud stream-of-consciousness give and take with himself as he seeks to find a way to elicit approval from his audience. There is no sense of sharing or listening in his style. He is the smartest person in the room, someone who knows more about science than the researchers, more about atomic weapons than the military strategists, and more about trade deals than the economists.

Perhaps the way to put it is not that his character mattered more than his predecessors' did, but that to an extreme degree bordering (if not transgressing) on the pathological, his own disposition shaped policy outcomes that were completely out of synch with the standards and boundaries of administrative norms, especially during a national crisis. This can be seen in his fascination with ratings, his constant need to talk himself up, to demean women of achievement in Congress and the media, and his embrace of foreign dictators on the basis of a certain superficial "simpatico" that has nothing to do with policy fit and longstanding alliance interests and everything to do with what he thinks they think of him and how "nice" they can be to each other. All of this drives his policy choices—to the neglect of professional advisory staffs in the intelligence community and the public health community—and sets him apart from almost all other U.S. politicians, placing him in a category with some of the most notorious of world leaders in history, many with blood on their hands.

The brazenness with which Trump stood in front of reputable epidemiologists like Dr. Anthony Fauci, longtime director of the National Institute of Allergy and Infectious Diseases, and Dr. Deborah Birx, U.S. Global AIDS Coordinator and Coordinator for the White House Coronavirus Task Force, and contradicted them, ignored them, taunted them and suggested absolutely ridiculous ideas about bleach or hydroxychloroquine as remedies, requires a level of chutzpah and disdain that virtually no president before has ever possessed. And to do so in the face of disastrous public health numbers, with outcomes consistently putting the lie to even the most roseate projections and expressions of hopeful outcomes, requires an intense degree of unselfconscious bravado and shamelessness.

It is important to keep this element in mind, because the behavior he modelled became internalized at virtually every level of government—through his subordinates at the cabinet- and political-appointee levels, as well as to the career politicians who sought his favor and needed to curry the support of Republican Party stalwarts through the nominations process. This includes senators, representatives, and a crucial if previously overlooked component of the transmission process by which policy is made and disseminated nationally—state governors.

It would be more accurate to say that the governors play a crucial role in compensating for the lack of national policy. One of the remarkable features of U.S. pandemic policy was the deliberate refusal to formulate a national plan and instead to let decisions and supply procurement policy devolve to the state level. It would be tempting to chalk this up to a predilection for "states' rights"—part of the conservative agenda's much-vaunted distrust of centralized power. But the peculiar part of that ideological penchant for positioning authority is how selective and arbitrary the decision is to let policy sit at the state level rather than with the national sovereign state. On matters of voting-rights enforcement, the Trump Administration was fine allowing states to determine everything from access to polls to ease of registration, criteria for absentee voting and whether felons who completed their sentences are to be granted rights at all. But on matters of state and municipal collaboration with agents from U.S. Immigration and Customs Enforcement the federal approach takes precedence, to the point where dissenting states and cities were threatened with a withdrawal of funding for non-compliance with policies targeting undocumented immigrants. The same for school districts and statewide education departments that, under the threat of COVID, withheld reopening classrooms out of an abundance of caution; they faced the possibility of federal funds being withdrawn; or at least that is how the Trump Administration framed its initial policy directives when the issue of school re-openings for the fall of 2020 became a matter of public debate.

In the case of public policy toward the pandemic, the administration took an extremely loose approach, abdicating any federally coordinated responsibility and leaving the states to fend for themselves—all while delegitimizing national healthcare efforts and data gathering.

The one area where the administration did attempt a hard line, predictably enough, was in trying to impose a Maginot Line defense of keeping out people from select countries. This is precisely the kind of mechanical, physical border wall isolationism that the Trump Administration touted elsewhere, along its southern border, and in a patchwork effort to keep out terrorists from primarily Islamic states—with equal ineffectiveness.

The appeal of such an approach is easy to understand. Its chief virtue is that it evolves from a mechanical, quasi-military policing model that entails no political reserves of legitimacy among the citizenry; it is a solution seemingly imposed from above, by the federal government and its combined military-police-intelligence-surveillance machinery. Unfortunately, it also does not work given the complex way in which a virus infiltrates a country with inherently fluid travel as part of its core being. When you are dealing with an infectious disease, it does not take much of a breach or leak for the virus to have an impact through transmission. There is no military-style sealant available.

It might well be part of a uniquely American strategic culture to see public policy and public health solutions in terms of clean, technical, quasi-military interventions that produce results without involving the messiness of human values or morals (Klein 1994). Certainly, the structure of U.S. involvement worldwide has borne this trait as a projection of its internalized sense of American Exceptionalism. We fight our wars "over there." We send the troops in to fix a problem. We keep the homeland safe and secure and rely upon our relative geographic isolation—protected on both flanks by vast oceans—to avoid the messiness of the recurring warfare and conflict that have so marred the history of Europe, Africa, Asia and Central America. In this sense a strategic approach to a pandemic is to search for a technical intervention that keeps the problem offshore.

Except we are not that different from other countries when it comes to the insidious dynamics of a viral epidemic. As the previous administration attempted to warn the incoming Trump Administration, fending off an infectious disease of any sort takes hard work, careful preparation, coordinated national policy and the behavioral cooperation of the citizenry to act in disciplined ways. None of that suits a regime based upon personal fealty, arbitrary decision making, mistrust of science and contempt for its own population—including its own electoral supporters.

To say the least, we are still not getting good role-model behavior from some of our political leaders. At one point, Tennessee Governor Bill Lee imposed partial restrictions on business activity and travel, but withheld a full shelter-in-place decree because he said he was concerned about preserving "personal freedoms." As if a society were even possible without some self-discipline and understanding of what it means to live with other people. At the risk of stating the obvious, that is the whole point of risk-reduction measures like speed limits, seat belt laws and stop signs.

Much of this, sadly, is to be expected from a country that has the lowest voter turnout of any industrial democracy: according to the U.S. Census Bureau, 61 percent of the voting-age eligible population in 2016 and 67 percent in 2020. That higher number in turnout amidst a pandemic suggests a level of voter arousal that indicates impressive mobilization. Nonetheless, the rate is comparatively low compared to other advanced democracies. Not coincidentally, we also have the least-developed system of national healthcare of all comparable democracies. When it comes to ensuring personal security, the United States relies upon privatized health insurance more than any other country. In addition, Americans own more guns per capita than any of our democratic cohorts. Small wonder that gun shops have been deemed "essential services" in state after state and we see long lines outside these stores as Americans prepare for some last-ditch defense should things really turn desperate in terms of domestic unrest.

None of which bodes well for the sensible measures required to ride out the ensuing storm as the country shifted its emphasis from "masks on" to "needles in the arm." What was true for social distancing held true for vaccinations. In the case of masks, something like 80 percent compliance went a long way toward flattening the curve; compliance at 50 or 60 percent had considerably less effect and kept us on a steady course to an overloaded hospital system and a death toll now exceeding all of the overseas wars the United States has ever fought. There is no way to estimate what our compliance rate was with social distancing. But it was certainly not three-quarters effective. Besides, a dam that is only 75 percent effective does not do a lot of good.

The casualness with which mask wearing was adopted, and the way it immediately became politicized into a tacit endorsement of one political party over another, reveals a lot about public volatility today. The issue plays into the same kind of intensive social anxiety that fuels claims by anti-vaxers that their refusal to take a medical precaution they see as dangerous should not disqualify them from mixing with those—comprising the majority—who accept at face value the scientific merits of vaccination. At least in the case of that community it could be said that their position is only medically tenable when they are "free riders" benefitting from the willingness of the overwhelming majority to get protection. In the case of mask wearing and social distancing as precautions to fend off transmission and infection, the debates became more complicated because a major component of the behavior involves a social commitment to the well-being of others. With face masks, after all, the issue had to do with donning them primarily to prevent the wearer from spreading the virus to others—a built-in relationship of social responsibility whose inherent appeal is a more complex web of other-regarding connections and moral sensibilities than is usually the case when citizens are asked to take precautions on the basis of self-interest.

In the case of texting or using a cellphone while motoring, the concern about distracted driving has a strong component of self-interest built in. There is certainly a measure of other-regarding behavior as well; the appeal to avoid getting into traffic accidents means a concern for passengers, other drivers and pedestrians. The appeal to oneself is pre-eminent, however. More so for wearing seat belts, where the appeal is entirely toward self-interest and an activity for which 80 percent compliance is considered a rousing success.

The same could be said for "don't text and drive" ordinances. While scarcely enforced and with no reliable data available as to compliance, they are still based upon appeals to the person behind the wheel. Moreover, there is no countervailing messaging from federal authorities or celebrities attesting to the value of "texting while driving." Nor does one find anyone willing to speak out openly about the value and messaging inherent in "drinking while driving."

It is interesting how sentiments against mask wearing, maintaining social distance and getting vaccinated converge with a longstanding heritage of rugged individualism and argument about self-sufficiency. Moreover, they have become part of a nativist discourse of public identity, one rooted in an anti-intellectual, crackpot kind of streetwise sensibility that flies in the face of science and education. There are powerful antecedents to this in American history, dating back to nineteenth century populism, and affirmed more recently through a fragmented national media structure that promotes self-reinforcing "silos" of belief. The country has long provided fervent ground for all sorts of crackpot movements, whether just strange or outright dangerous: everything from the Know-Nothing party to the Ku Klux Klan, Scientology or school boards insisting on creationism over evolution as the basis for science teaching, What is unique about the turn that public discourse has increasingly taken of late is the intensity of the resulting passions, the self-certainty of believers, and the fatal consequences of adhering to norms that defy the public good. When the rejection of scientific norms gets wrapped up in a Confederate flag and then goes out "en marche" armed with automatic weaponry in an effort to reclaim its version of freedom—in the process overtaking a state legislative session like Michigan's or Oregon's, to the point where the legislators have to flee the building—then we are entering into a realm of mobilized, militarized dynamics that make politics all but impossible.

Complicating matters was the way President Trump interpreted mask wearing: a sign of public endorsement of him. In typically Trumpian terms he personalized the issue into a referendum on his own likeability rather than a public health issue or a statement—if that is what it was at all—about a citizen's sense of risk tolerance and aversion.

It is obviously harder for some populations to adhere to the necessary norms of isolation because of unsteady, ill-paying employment and lack of adequate healthcare coverage. It takes the ability to stockpile food, for example, and to rely upon delivery services rather than recurring trips to the grocery. That presumes a measure of cash reserves to be able to buy in bulk. It also presumes enough space at home for storing provisions and keeping kids occupied. Access to the Internet is notoriously limited by virtue of economic class, for example. Without that access there is no on-line learning. There is an inherent class bias to being able to handle stay-at-home resolutions.

There are also deep cultural biases that come into play about wearing a mask, or not. For American Blacks, for example, wearing a mask raises a distinct threat to their safety. Given the level of police violence against the Black community and the suspicion under which so many Blacks immediately fall for being in "the wrong neighborhood" or looking suspicious because they are wearing a hoodie or some sort of face covering, wearing a mask can induce profound anxiety and uncertainty. This is one of those searing issues of race relations that needs to be examined and that has only begun to be discussed as part of the Black Lives Matter movement. What is interesting for now in this context of the politics of mask wearing is the palpable difference in behavior between those participating in public rallies against police brutality and those attending Trump rallies.

As seen in late June/early July 2020 with Trump gatherings in Tulsa, Phoenix and at Mt. Rushmore, mask wearing was distinctly frowned upon, discouraged and considered open defiance of the norms embodied in the rally. Picture, by contrast, the vast throngs of protestors assembled and marching across the country in the name of Black Lives Matter and against police brutality, where the anecdotal evidence is overwhelming of mask wearing, if not exactly social distancing.

The iconography is not hollow; it carries significant political weight. The public protests are other-regarding. The Trump rallies affirm an entirely insular sensibility.

Social distancing, mask wearing and submitting to inoculation require that a measure of self-discipline be imparted and internalized. That requires appropriate modeling from our leaders. It also requires a larger public commitment to the ethos of public virtue over atomistic freedom. And, beyond making moral demands, it also requires the availability of a basic net of mutual social support. Without that we are in serious trouble.

That is the same nature and complexity of the demands we face as the shift takes place from cloth and paper face coverings to induced immunity via injection. The curiosity here is that the voluntary compliance runs in several directions, and with somewhat more intense consequences than the case with simple masking and social distance. This time around the compliance is more directly epidemiological. Citizens are on their own as to whether to opt for the vaccine. Suspicions about the government's "real" intent will suppress participation; indeed, there were rumors circulating through right-wing social media sites almost immediately after initial emergency approval of the vaccine by the Centers for Disease Control and Prevention (CDC) that some sort of monitor would be implanted in the brains of those who got the vaccine—a suspicion that persisted long after full official CDC approval. This is in addition to a certain percentage of the populace that simply does not trust anything the government does, plus those who do not believe in science. A certain space will also always be occupied by those claiming various religious objections to inoculation. Others will claim invulnerability to the virus or are simply afraid to get any sort of injection and figure they can become free riders to herd immunity. Stranger, still, are those who repudiate the science behind the vaccines but have no qualms about ingesting a demonstrably dangerous horse deworming medicine, Ivermectin, to fend off COVID-19.

To some extent, even the utility of the vaccine has been marginally compromised by the difficulty of requiring a vaccine passport that would grant bearers a kind of "open transit" to relatively closed, exclusive gatherings like concerts, sporting events, restaurants and air travel. The efficiency of such a passport would considerably ease the uncertainty of life in a post-pandemic world. But the deep-seated, almost libertarian reluctance to allow such a government-issued pass (which at least one genius Congressperson likened to a Nazi-era yellow Jewish star) imperiled plans for such documentation. Instead, the country has been forced to rely upon voluntary acknowledgement, with the curious proviso that those who admit they are *not* vaccinated still being expected to wear a mask and uphold social distance. Yet this is the last group of demographic sectors likely to admit to wearing masks. Conversely, those citizens embodying extreme caution are the most likely to continue wearing masks and exhibiting caution in intimate indoor settings; and in the process, because they are precisely the ones who persist in wearing masks, they are also likely to arouse suspicions of not being vaccinated.

An effort to promote public safety through other-regarding behavior thus yields an ironic reversal in appearances, with the least virtuous evading their duty in a double sense, while the most virtuous arouse suspicions of recalcitrance and concern that they must be avoided in public spaces of a would-be democracy.

Bibliography

Applebaum, A. (2021) *Twilight of Democracy: The Seductive Lure of Authoritarianism*, New York: Anchor.

Gessen, M. (2020) *Surviving Autocracy*, New York: Riverhead Books.

Kendzior, S. (2020) *Hiding in Plain Sight: The Invention of Donald Trump and the Erosion of America*, New York: Flatiron Books.

Klein, B. (1994) *Strategic Studies and World Order: The Global Politics of Deterrence*, Cambridge: Cambridge University Press.

Levitsky, S. and D. Ziblatt (2019) *How Democracies Die*, New York: Crown Publishers.

Snyder, T. (2017) *On Tyranny: Lessons from The Twentieth Century*, New York: Tim Duggan Books.

Stanley, J. (2020) *How Fascism Works: The Politics of Us and Them*, New York: Random House.

3
MEDIA

Just as it is impossible to imagine Mussolini or Hitler coming to power without radio, it is hard to disentangle Donald Trump from the prevailing social media landscapes of our time, particularly Twitter and Facebook. Likewise, it is impossible to imagine the emergence of Trump as a celebrity/businessman/politician without Fox News and right-wing talk radio—both of which established themselves as leaders in the emergence of niche audience marketing. In fact, the way in which Trump came to dominate the news cycle is not just attributable to his own facility in presenting a façade, or to those of his partisan supporters who set out to exploit him as a phenomenon. The mainstream press—including daily newspapers, network news and cable TV coverage—found in his candidacy and in his persona a mechanism for a ratings bonanza that was the contemporary equivalent of the old battles between city newspapers for local circulation and sales. This modern nexus—of Trump as social media platform, object of fawning coverage and of total dominance of the news cycle—deserves attention, not only for what it enabled, but also for what is made difficult to achieve: a critical, independent citizenry able to form its own judgments and able to see through the fog of propaganda, manufactured news and public relations.

To understand how Trump both mesmerized and paralyzed the traditional press while mobilizing the news media, it is crucial to backtrack a bit and explore analytically the changing structure of media. It is important to point out that Trump emerged as a darling of facile press coverage. He was also someone who was always far more volatile and blunt in his crassness than he was credited with. And he was a very appealing subject of constant coverage on a 24/7 news cycle. To a large degree, what counts as the mainstream press (major cable television networks, national newspapers and news weeklies) worked strenuously to normalize him as a politician and sought to paper over his extremism. His excesses

DOI: 10.4324/9781003268741-4

were there from the start in terms of misogyny, racism and his revulsion of media and their criticisms, democratic norms and accountability; likewise, his contempt for the poor and the physically disabled, a penchant for lawlessness and personal vendettas and violence as ways of dealing with people and problems rather than through civilized discourse.

The news media celebrated Trump for his outrage and for the audience he brought to the fold through a kind of recursive circularity spawned by whatever outlandish things he said or did. Followers retweeted, responses generated responses, and he became a viral sensation in a new media ecosystem with its innumerable feedback loops on a regular basis. The media organizations helped him build an audience in the process and empowered people to participate in opinion formation and circulation without any of his statements requiring vetting. Few had the slightest idea what was really being said or what the basis was for adjudicating among competing claims about events. Masha Gessen (2020) has dubbed Trump's verbal assertions "word piles," an apt characterization of verbiage that appears designed to name, pronounce judgment and condemn, and which focuses on any number of injustices done to the one consistent subject of his rants (himself) rather than explaining and making explicit arguments and analysis (Gessen 2020: 94). The result was that citizens who used to follow politics now had to make way for the coverage of a celebrity who was never quite held accountable for his views, his actions or his lies. In the late-nineteenth century, the French sociologist Gustave LeBon wrote what became a virtual handbook for public tyrants, *The Crowd*, in which he argued that the key to mobilizing an electoral crowd was "affirmation, repetition, contagion" (LeBon 1896: 115). Flash forward twelve decades: the media did precisely that work *for* Trump.

Trump had long enjoyed a curious capacity to both dominate the news cycle and actually avoid having to be taken seriously as an object of sustained inquiry. Part of this was rooted in his long history of media savvy, a skill he honed in the 1970s while establishing himself among local New York media circles loosely concerned with business and real estate. It was a skill he would go on to deploy as his business portfolio grew, even during the phase of serial bankruptcies that plagued his overextended portfolio decades later, before he was rescued financially and in terms of status by the ratings bonanza of the network TV show he hosted, "The Apprentice."

What better way to master the art of public reputation building than by forging close relationships with those who would actually do most of the reporting and editing? A structural analysis of the media industry alone would not suffice to capture the peculiar capacity of a career charlatan to seduce and hoodwink the American and, in many cases, even the world press. Yet, without this level of radical idiosyncrasy and outsized personality we miss out on some of his unique characteristics: the ability of this peculiar historical figure to emerge from the pack, so to speak, and commandeer our attention and the reins of power.

At one level, the tools of a keen propagandist are not difficult to discern. Whether Trump acquired these through careful study of the past (doubtful), stumbling upon them accidentally (possible) or simply as a result of coincidental synergy between an extreme narcissistic personality and the character of modern news making (likely), the pattern has been there from the beginning. It helps to be comfortable lying, whether on small things or on big ones, and it also helps to be so shameless and unaware of one's own complicity in deceiving the audience that at the end of the day you yourself cannot distinguish between what you have said and what occupies a space outside of oneself that has its own material reality. It also helps if you have no regard for the kinds of character traits that normally constitute everyday discourse, such as continuity of identity, values about things that are beyond yourself, much less a shred of commitment to the sensitivities of other people. If you are entirely solipsistic and self-regarding, and if you are all wrapped up in your own insecurities, endlessly seeking affirmation from others by virtue of constant assertions of your own genius and achievements, then it becomes impossible to engage in what might be termed "accepted political discourse" because there is nothing there with which to engage except an act of will. This is dissociated man—a man for and with whom a politics is simply impossible.

What complicates matters is the extent to which Trump would personally go to establish intimate working relations with members of the media, then rely upon those relationships for favorable coverage that never probed very far below the surface of his accepted appeal of the outrageous and the outlandish. It was a skill he perfected during the gossip-page saturated era of metro-New York coverage, most notoriously the *New York Post*'s Page Six. Trump was not the least averse to calling reporters on their cellphones with stories, trial balloons for plans, or simply to compliment them on a recent article—often sending via fax or surface mail a copy of the article with his favorable comments scrawled across it, usually accompanied by his virtually illegible signature in black sharpie. (One of us, during an extended stint as a golf writer, was the recipient of many of these, along with the indulgent offers and treatment that went with them). Nor was he reluctant to voice his complaints, often in loud, uncompromising droning nasal tones that had less to do with the substance of the article in question than simply need to voice his own wildly biased views on the subject.

Trump treated reporters like domestic partners in an abusive relationship, fawning on them, flattering them, then abusing them verbally, warning them about a possible professional breach or going over their heads to their editors and publishers, threatening to pull ads or to expose perceived failures or what he thought might be conflicts of interest.

Trump was known to invite reporters to accompany him on trips, either on his personal airplanes when he was "just" a businessman, or on Air Force One when he became president. The expectation of favorable coverage was always there. There was also an element of the seduction of power for a reporter to be granted access and proximity to the intimate workings of decision-making, even if it all was a carefully calculated ploy designed to elicit favorable press coverage. The results grew into a blur of attention, compounded by the realization that the relationship was entirely exploitive and one-sided and subject to his severance upon perception of the slightest reluctance to play along. Sometimes the retribution came behind the scenes. Increasingly, during his presidency the rebukes were issued publicly, the bulk of them against female reporters for whom he reserved a special scorn that in most cases was indistinguishable from outright misogyny. Those familiar with the dynamics of domestic abuse will immediately recognize the parallels here with Trump's media behavior.

These skills Trump learned in hucksstering, blustering and mob-bossing his way around to cultivate an image in the relative intimacy of nightlife, real estate, golf and hospitality—venues where he initially practiced the same skills he took to the national and international stage when he became a presidential aspirant. What was different this time was that the lies and hatred he spawned had real consequences for real people outside the immediate circles of media production and circulation.

Lying about your achievements (or failures) is one thing; it is quite another to implicate others in ways that victimize vulnerable people while you suspend your own accountability for the viciousness that quickly sets in. Reckless accusations launched against the Central Park Five, for example. Birtherism about President Barack Obama. Dismissing Mexicans as racists and criminals. Invoking "Lock Her Up" as punishment for Hillary Clinton's emails. Dismissing talk about rape as casual locker-room banter. Each became a kind of trial run as to what he could get away with. The media—increasingly transfixed by the spectacle he posed and worried about appearing to be unbalanced or partisan in its coverage by engaging too critically the lies that undergirded these claims—ended up paralyzed; or worse, they normalized this discourse of threat and intimidation by reducing it to standard electoral tactics and the conventional jockeying for positions that marks a competitive, two-party race. In effect, they legitimized his candidacy and his entire approach to politics. In the process, violent politics were normalized in turn.

Trump's rallies were often livestreamed by cable TV with next to no effort made to fact check or counter his angry, rambling speeches. The viciousness of tone was explained away as "Trump being Trump." Liberal commentators frequently attributed his vulgarity to his being a political neophyte, with assurances that he would probably mature into the job as the institution of the presidency ultimately constrained him. Or, at worst, he would be kept in line by the "adults in the room," who would manage him and steer him into becoming a responsible politician.

Caught off guard by his unexpected election in November 2016, the mainstream press generally bent over backwards to make amends for their neglect of his supporters by heading off into small-town America to make inquiries into the nature and depths of his support. Meanwhile, Trump continued his assault on the media as a whole, and on press freedoms in particular, by denouncing their coverage, humiliating reporters by name at his largely ceremonial press conferences and reverting to public displays of his power through televised cabinet meetings while restricting much of his decision-making to a small internal corps of loyalists that usually included his daughter and son-in-law.

Meanwhile, those "dress rehearsal lies" from the campaign morphed into bigger and more consequential lies once the administration took hold. Viewers were presented with test runs to see how far Trump could go—and revealing how little pushback he would get from the press. It all started with Inaugural Day 2017, when Trump falsely claimed—with the help of his press secretary at the first White House press conference—that his inauguration had drawn a bigger crowd than Obama had eight years earlier. Many of the lies that followed would be classified as stupid and pointless—except that the need to assert them, and then the follow up effort to make them appear *true*, belied a deeper, darker agenda. The strategy became one of curtailing peoples' capacity to distinguish truth from fiction, all the while asserting his new political brand as being so contrary to anything else on offer that it was the willingness to be outlandish that became the story, not the short-circuiting of critical analysis relative to what was happening to political discourse.

Trump made an inappropriately political speech to a national Boy Scout jamboree in July 2017, and then falsely claimed the organization's leadership told him it was the greatest talk they had ever hosted. He claimed having been named Michigan's Man of the Year when there was no such award. In 2017, when he mistakenly indicated that the path of a hurricane might reach Alabama—despite what all professional meteorologists were saying—he had the National Oceanic Atmospheric Administration come to the Oval Office to show retroactively redrawn maps that "proved" he had been perspicacious when in fact he was just blithering. He deceptively claimed that wind turbine noise caused cancer, and that he helped bring back Midwest university football after the Big 10 announced a momentary halt due to the pandemic in 2020. He said he was unaware of a $130,000 payment to silence a porn star over an alleged affair, even when it became clear he specifically directed his attorney, Michael Cohen, to make the payment.

The lies, however, were not just isolated incidents. Nor were they just idiosyncratic—a case of "Trump being Trump." In retrospect we can see they were part of an accumulating strategy designed to unsettle the terms of American political discourse, mock those who were covering him and thereby sully the institution of a free press, showing the willingness of the public to believe just about anything, and eventually to lie his way into a second term.

Trump's promise to release his tax returns proved hollow, as did the claim that a new healthcare plan to replace the Affordable Care Act would be ready "in two weeks' time." In the first of two massive lies that would ultimately prove to mark the start of his undoing, he claimed on February 26, 2020, that the "virus is under control." And later that year, when he lost the general election to Joe Biden, he began to mount the campaign of the "Big Lie" by contesting the validity of the results and his loss by over seven million votes.

It cannot be claimed with any certainty that had the media acted differently and reported in a more investigative and critical manner the whole phenomenon of Trump could have been avoided. That is an abstract counterfactual at best; and in any case we will never know. But what can be said here is that throughout his campaign and during the bulk of his presidency the press generally did an awful job of peeling back the layers of deception to reveal the underlying chaos of decision-making, not to mention the mendacity of Trump and several principals in his administration. The press failed to give the American public the depth and breadth of information and analysis needed to make judgments about what was actually going on. They also betrayed the underlying function of the press, which is to bring light into dark shadows of power and to provide perspective and an understanding of alternatives so that citizens might make sound judgments. What we got, instead, was a lot of superficial coverage that normalized Trump and fell back on the fallacy of false equivalence between the two political parties when it came to tactics. What the press missed was the extent to which the intent of the Trump Administration was to dismantle governance and the rule of law. This provided the cloak for reallocating federal resources in ways that fundamentally benefited the extremely wealthy, large corporate interests, extractive industries, white supremacists and nativists while attacking peoples of color, the LGBTQ communities, immigrants and the poor.

There were a few notable exceptions, such as a *New York Times* expose of some of his tax records; or *Washington Post* stories about his negligence with his eponymous charities and real estate holdings. But in their editorial coverage of White House doings even these media organizations were reluctant, if not altogether evasive, on the issue of "lies" big and small, using instead more sedate and less trenchant terminology like "misrepresentation" or "unfounded." The *New York Times*, in particular, bent over backwards in its op-ed pages, giving considerable space to conservative columnists—a strategy that comported with the paper's overall concern not to appear biased or antagonistic toward the kinds of readership that would have been inclined to support Trump. Even their inside reporting on White House politics and jockeying among aides for the president's attention reduced the entirety of the picture to "insider baseball" coverage—strong on personalities and intrigue where the emphasis was on the political gaming and norms of bargaining, rather than on a more nuanced, structural picture of the extent of the deviation from everyday norms. By the time they caught up to the insidious nature of the president's lies after the November 2020 election, the damage was done and the image and the many falsehoods he told had found a place secure from any rational argument or inquiry.

How it is possible to hide in plain sight (Kendzior 2020) can only be understood by exploring the altered media landscape that the Trump candidacy and presidency occupied. To do so is to learn some powerful lessons about what journalism and the media can do to help promote a healthy democracy.

Of course, traditional media outlets like daily newspapers, and even the more critical coverage afforded by the likes of *The New Yorker* and *The Atlantic* magazines, paled in comparison to the ability of social media outlets like Twitter and Facebook to traffic in rumors, innuendo, falsehoods, blatant lies and conspiracy theories without any pretense of restraint. For example, at his peak on Twitter, with some 80 million followers, Trump was able to reach a much larger audience than through any of the conventional outlets—far surpassing even the self-selected audience of acolytes who watched his every word being affirmed on Fox News all day long.

We have some evidence of what a different media culture might look like from the days immediately following the January 6, 2021, attempted coup on Congress. In the immediate aftermath of Trump's inciting the riot, both Twitter and Facebook shut down his accounts. Amazon also shut down Parler, the preferred right-wing mode of digital communication. Over the next ten days, the digital media watchdog Zignal Labs reported a 73 percent decrease in the trafficking of misinformation, lies and conspiracy theories regarding the election (*Washington Post*, January 16, 2021). Meanwhile, independent researchers—online watchdog groups like Bellingcat—started vacuuming up as much open-source, online digital material in videos, photos, messages and selfies from YouTube, Snapchat, Instagram, TikTok, Twitter and Facebook that had been posted by conspirators and rioters. They turned to digital archives like Reddit and Intelligence X as well as to standard Google searches in their sweep of the material. The effort to document the siege and to identify participants produced a flood of information that was turned over to the FBI and other authorities in the hunt for those responsible (Burgess 2021): "Open-source sleuths are already unmasking the Capitol Hill mob". This had, after all, been a viral conspiracy, organized on social media in advance and livestreamed while in progress, so that a considerable trail of evidence remained, even as those who had been involved attempted to delete the digital trail they left behind. In some cases, surreptitiously utilized dating platforms like Bumble, Tinder and Match were deployed to solicit self-profiled conservative Republicans or alt-right people to gain their confidence, encourage their self-disclosure and accumulate boastful examples of their having participated in the riot, which the digital Mata Haris (and Mata Harrys) dutifully turned over to government officials searching for rioters they could identify.

Commentators and would-be news analysts abound in print, on television and on an increasing number of social media platforms. Too many place a primacy on being brazen, outrageous and self-promoting. The caustic voices that proliferate have an inherent advantage. With so few barriers to entry, anything that can be posted quickly gets registered in the form of "clicks" that generate self-referential algorithms designed to effect attention and seem also to summon forth a call to action. The result—what is called search engine optimization in the parlance of media business managers—becomes an end unto itself, carrying with it powerful political consequences that are wholly new, and many of them potentially dangerous. Editors come to judge writers on the basis of the clicks their work draws. Headlines are chosen for their suitability to attention-getting rather than to their specific focus on the article. Reporters come to judge their own self-worth on the basis of clicks and start picking—and rejecting—topics to write about based upon their suitability in terms of attracting attention.

Here is one possible consequence, which we venture as a hypothesis. In a media culture that thrives on conflict, perhaps Americans today are not politically polarized so much as they are accustomed to being told again and again that political polarization is the defining feature of our political time. Having come to view it as a natural outgrowth of a distinct political era—through countless incentives and rewards—the ensuing polarization seems not to be the consequence of individuals' pre-given attitudes, but instead the outcome of media-driven forces that push the envelope of the reasonable and the rational, working in lockstep with incentive mechanisms that facilitate the intensification of opinions and attitudes of the new media mechanisms themselves. How can democratic aptitude survive, much less inhere within such a culture?

From a vast and rapidly growing literature in media studies we have learned to question how to grapple with the crush of the everyday world of events. At the same time, those who have been the subject matter of media coverage have increasingly gained new resources to help shape their own public identities and actions. At one level, that means becoming media savvy in learning how to use news coverage to cultivate a desired image. It is a skill for the political arts whose value became readily apparent as far back as 1960. When Nixon and Kennedy debated that year, the two presidential candidates sparred, with Nixon winning the older demographic radio audience and Kennedy sweeping the television viewers. JFK proved more "telegenic," a capacity that subsequent candidates came to cultivate as a necessary aesthetic. The ability to manufacture one's public identity for political purpose had been central to a certain populist movie genre, from *Mr. Deeds Goes to Town* (1936) and *Mr. Smith Goes to Washington* (1939) to *A Face in the Crowd* (1957). But those films were more about a certain accidentally acquired trait rather than a skill that was studied, learned, honed and mastered. The dark side of this construction was revealed in *The Manchurian Candidate* (1962), where the focus was on the unwitting bearer of an identity he does not even know he has, much less how he got it. It took Joe McGinnis's *The Selling of the President* (1969) to provide the how-to handbook for cynical public identity so that political candidates could learn how to stand before the media and produce something akin to the desired public-relations effect.

As if a classic distinction could ever be delineated between the source of coverage and the object of inquiry, today's mediatization of the world has blurred the lines between news coverage and performance, between perspective and identity formation. The endless cycle of creative production makes it impossible to distinguish cause and effect, genesis and dispersal. The result is liberating in some respects. Yet, in another, it undercuts the ability to discern basic truth from manufactured fiction. It makes possible the temptation to engage in big lies in the mistaken assumption that anything is possible, and that anything can be papered over and tagged with a label convenient to aspiring partisans—even something as delusional as "Trump won the 2020 election." One need not be committed to objectivism to understand that in such a world, almost anything becomes possible, or at least tempting. If that were truly achievable, we would have nothing but a war of words and images, a constructed realm of sheer will assertion. This dynamic becomes especially important, as we will explain, in the context of fascism.

Politics and civil society require a discipline and a level of commitment that restrain the unlimited violence inherent in the position that all "truths" are possible, and that lies, whether big or small, acquire a level of validity if they are attached to adequate power.

In a context in which media coverage is both produced and contested, the stakes are raised higher than ever for those responsible for creating and reporting content. News journalists in particular have to be mindful of the process by which issues arise as newsworthy and are framed by the participants. It is not enough to rely upon the old journalism-school cliché of "who-what-when-how-where-why" as a basis of story construction. It is also not feasible to rely on the canard that one needs to set aside one's point of view or values entirely in order to write truthfully.

The practice of journalism entails an underlying commitment to the value of getting a story right and to informing a citizenry that needs the truth in order to fulfill its function of holding leaders accountable for their actions. Those are constitutive values of the practice, not ancillary constraints that somehow make media coverage biased. While it is never a good idea to approach a story or an issue with preconceived ideas of who is right and who is wrong, it is necessary to make judgments all along about who is being truthful about what and whether all possible sides to the story require equal billing as equally valid. It is also important for journalists to vet secondary and tertiary claims predicated on what "some people are saying." To be sure, not all accounts are equally valid and not all perspectives merit anywhere close to equal weight. Particularly when people in power make claims that would favor their side or tend to enhance their power and position, it is the inherent job of journalists to proceed critically, with abundant skepticism and great caution. As we will see, a self-imposed professional reluctance to proceed critically within a media culture that lionized performative showmanship and bravado greatly hindered the journalistic community in assessing and foreseeing the full scope of the Trumpian initiative until it was (almost) too late. In the war that some have waged against the media, mainstream journalistic outlets cowered, allowing alternative, less responsible outlets to take over. The result was a decline in the quality and availability of journalism, which has fed authoritarian tendencies and enabled more violent partisanships to gain a firm foothold in the political culture. At the end of the day, and perhaps inadvertently, the media made Trump more than he ever was by framing him as an acceptable politician and by devaluing the extent to which his aspirational program violated longstanding democratic norms.

When it comes to vetting a version of truth or reasonableness, nothing is less suited to careful sifting and evaluation of terms than the frenetic cycle introduced by social media. They function as platforms of opinion, rumor, self-expression and witticism as well as barbed takedowns and bullying, but not as quasi-public arenas for mutual engagement and discourse. What a decade or two ago was heralded as shared space of "virtual community" has become at one level a venue for unfettered expression and at another level a highly profitable business that manages to cash in on the availability of personal data through algorithms that enable the platform owners a means to sell those data to companies seeking to reach a specific demographic or subculture. The result is less a forum than a chaotic marketplace with no rules or standards for engagement. While individual citizens can use it to share in their feelings, circumstances and personal experience, the medium lends itself very quickly to those with a partisan agenda seeking to arouse sentiments and mobilize support. Because the medium also enables participants to build through self-selection their own silos of communication and what counts as community, the result is anything but public enlightenment: it is closer to a shoving match that favors the strongest opinions and the loudest voices.

A whole new media universe has thus found a secure place as an alternative to the mainstream. Flourishing in various guises, it sports digital news platforms, social media connectivity, web platforms, Podcasts, talk radio, chat rooms, video posting and any number of apps. Some of them are protected by vast corporate interests for their profitability; others flourish because of their ease of access and appeal to a particular age or identity group. There has been a notorious reluctance by the companies running these sites to censor material for fear of appearing political; also, to do so would create a precedent for monitoring the kinds of activities that are the basis of the business model that has seen advertisers able to reach, with greater efficiency than ever, an intended audience of consumers.

Twitter and Facebook have their own unique dynamic built in, one that contributes to what might best be called a high noise-to-signal ratio. The business model is based on reinforcing the choices of those who log on, determined by their proclivity to follow certain subgroups or lifestyle genres and then via feedback loops to provide commercial affirmation via targeted ads tailored as narrowly as possible to particular inclinations. In the hands of an assertive social media practitioner the results mean an extreme "siloing" of affect, especially when the voices are reinforced by bots and other back-channel followers and posters that highjack the process of community building by reinforcing and multiplying the bias of the judgment through links, follows and repostings. Consequently, lies, rumors and deliberate misrepresentations gain currency and acquire discursive legitimacy.

Trump understood the power he could wield if he could master all of this, using Twitter, for example, to reach as many as 80 million followers before he was finally shut down in the aftermath of the January 6 attack on the Capitol. Until then he had spent much of his time as candidate and president bypassing traditional press conferences to unsheathe a daily blitz of venom, inuendo and misleading information. This took place against an accompanying campaign designed to enfeeble the public by disabling the trust mechanisms of traditional media sources, and in the process contribute to a culture in which any reporting not to his liking was dismissed as fake news. CNN was attacked for its "dishonest reporting." The mainstream media was reduced to "the lamestream media," a term he pulled from Sarah Palin a decade earlier. The *New York Times* was "a disgrace to journalism." Even before the November 2020 election, when Fox News made an early call on behalf of Arizona falling to Biden, Trump targeted his favorite cable outlet ("daytime is unwatchable," he tweeted). The unrelenting assault had a double effect: it spawned mistrust among those elements of the populace inclined to see Trump as their savior; and it put the targeted media outlets in a defensive, crouching posture so that a certain level of self-censorship in their coverage would develop and subsequently be put on autopilot.

Amidst this vortex of messaging and misinformation, the task of conveying news responsibly, accurately and fairly had become very difficult. For one thing, there are fewer editorial controls that mediate the production of the news and its distribution than there were a decade ago. The costs of doing business became a concern for the traditional media outlets, whether on TV or in print. The concerns became even more significant as corporate buyouts, consolidations and takeovers reduced staffing, led to newspaper closures, and encouraged corporate accountancy to rule over traditional care in the vetting of story production. There is nothing more expensive in journalism than doing a long-term, detailed investigation. It can occupy a team of reporters for a year, if it is to be done right. The payback in terms of journalistic integrity is considerable but, if stockholders are making the calls, then the impatience with a return on investment becomes considerable.

TV in particular has become far more fast-paced, with multiple images vying for viewers' attention and jangling the nerves as each demands constant attention. It is not uncommon to see a host on one side of the screen, a person or three interviewed on the other side, with a subhead announcing the immediate topic and a separate chyron running live underneath with yet more news bytes at odds with the substantive concerns of the main screen. Video clips are increasingly used as if on a carousel, with two or three five-second clips repeated in a rotation that feels like a revolving door that is spinning ever faster. Present this on a 24-hour basis, seven days a week, and what it does is accelerate the news cycle while making context, analysis and structure harder, if not impossible, for an audience to follow and comb through. The phenomenon is found across the cable news spectrum, whether on Fox News, CNN or MSNBC, although Fox News is more practiced in the technique of discombobulation than any of the others.

It should be said that media manipulation in the service of political power is not new to the Trump era. In the mid-1930s, European cultural critic Walter Benjamin diagnosed a troubling condition relative to the advent of modern artistic production. Benjamin was concerned about the alienation of art from the object itself in the context of its production and mass distribution. He worried that the audience's unique experience with the "aura" of an original work of art was being lost, and with it an understanding of the difference between the real and the copy or an imitation. The phenomenon he sought to diagnose would culminate in the fascist aesthetics that predominated in interwar Germany, Austria and Italy, though it also speaks to today's combination of Internet-driven digital drama and the hyperactive media coverage that is so much a part of network and cable television. Benjamin's immediate context was cinema, but the analysis remains directly relevant today because it highlights the way an object or performer with an authentic "aura" or sense of self in place becomes separated from the process of production and ends up yielding to a desired, rather than an intended, effect or narrative, one that is no longer able to stand on its own.

In what he characterized as "art in the age of mechanical reproduction," Benjamin decried the loss of perspective relative to the degradation of the "aura" of the authentic performance. The actor's body in film "loses its corporeality—it evaporates, it is deprived of reality, life, voice, and the noises caused by his moving about. The unique 'aura of the person' yields to the 'spell of the personality'" (Benjamin 2019: 224). For Benjamin, this dynamically constructed persona of the film character—as much the product of the film director and editor as of the actor him- or herself—creates a performative aestheticization that carries dangerous potential. It seeks to mobilize mass sentiment and create an object of common admiration without the audience bringing into question any of the social conditions by which the performance is constructed: for example, technical, economic or market mechanisms that lie behind the production of the art performance. In this process, Benjamin discerns the moment of a mass mobilization that is both creative and disabling at the same time. "But the instant the criterion of authenticity ceases to be applicable to artistic reproduction, the total function of art is reversed. Instead of being based on ritual, it begins to be based on another practice—politics" (2019: 224). The uncritical, mass politics that inculcates familiarity with the commonly accessible spurns innovation and challenge. Indeed, it turns innovation on its head and celebrates violence for its own sake without attaching it to instrumentality, to ends and means or to ideals beyond the aesthetic act itself. "Mechanical reproduction of art changes the reaction of the masses toward art. ... The conventional is uncritically enjoyed, and the truly new is criticized with aversion" (234).

What is the mass? For Benjamin it was a "matrix from which all traditional behavior toward works of art issues … in a new form. Quantity has been transmuted into quality. The greatly increased mass of participants has produced a change in the mode of participation" (239). "The public is an examiner, but an absent-minded one." The stakes could not be higher: "Fascism sees its salvation in giving the masses not their right, but instead a chance to express themselves" (241).

For Benjamin fascism represented something aesthetic through and through, and this was a foreboding development. "The logical result of Fascism is the introduction of aesthetics in political life.… All efforts to render politics aesthetics culminate in one thing: war" (241).

That is one reason—probably the main reason—that fascism is so difficult to identify, define and understand. Following Benjamin, fascism basically amounts to a *will* to pronounce meaning, however fleeting and however multiple the subtle acts of will assertion and imposition. For a period of time, it obliterates tradition while harnessing what can be made to count as traditional as long as the discourses, rhetoric and images can be put to work to eviscerate what would otherwise serve as context and circumstance. That which needs to be regarded critically through careful consideration and patient reflection is obliterated. Fascism lavishes attention and introduces a disorienting atmosphere of awe, amazement and fear. It is hypnotic and mesmerizing, spell binding, but also paralyzing.

Understanding of self, other and context in our challenging "postmodern" landscape requires deliberate acts of reframing how it is that media issues are presented to a would-be critical public. That includes examining from where those issues emerged and learning how they acquired traction in a particular political environment. Because so much of what constitutes the news buzz is framed according to a logic that violently isolates events, abstracting them from a dense social setting means treating each as a special case. Indeed, the very concept of "news" as something that happens above the normal din and patterning of everyday life ensures that some of the most significant trends will be overlooked in the name of covering "breaking news"—what is happening now. Context is reduced to fleeting links enabled by digital technologies and haptic design mechanisms, all of them aided and abetted by those all too willing to follow along within the consolidating knowledge streams of consciousness. Charting entirely new courses for thought and analysis, striving for spontaneity, independence and novelty— all necessary for a healthy democratic polity—all of this becomes exceedingly difficult.

These dynamics have received a great deal of attention over the past fifteen years, but the forces driving the accelerated speeds of ad-hoc interface behavior nonetheless continue and appear to be largely unstoppable. There are sturdy handholds to be grasped, however, and with creativity and imagination the forces behind the new mechanisms of conformity can be turned on their head and can lead people to understand themselves and their political worlds differently.

In the present political moment, the connections between authoritarian politics and the new digital media landscapes, especially those connections that emerge in the context of such radical proliferation of political discourse, require further examination. What responsibilities do today's media cultures place on citizens relative to acquiring information, developing fact-based knowledge, instilling a desire to think, question, reflect and participate in discussions that can deepen, enrich and enliven democratic politics?

The new media landscapes of our time are powerful cultural attractors. They are certainly known to be frenzied and harried. Perhaps they are also the chief instruments of political polarization. But are they much more than this? Could it be that they are instrument and effect at the same time? A case in point: claims that it was legitimate for legislators to raise objections to validating the results of the November 2020 election, and with it the Electoral College count, because millions of citizens had "concerns" about the legitimacy of the outcome. This justification deftly leaves out of the equation that it is precisely Trump and his supporters, while they constitute a minority of the electorate, who used social media to fan the flames of discontent and propagate lies about the outcome of the election. There may be no better case in recent years of media-driven polarization as both cause and effect.

Intensely held beliefs are said to be the order of the day. There can be little doubt these beliefs are replicated and amplified in countless media spaces—some old, though most quite new—that infiltrate so many facets of our lives. Consequently, many people come to understand that a dynamic like polarization is neither necessarily new nor unique. Polarization seems a reflection of the intensification of dynamics associated with the means for expressing beliefs that have created a new, complex situation—one that only further feeds the fire. Faced with the onslaught of encounters with what are presented as firm beliefs, so rock solid and stable they stand against the forces of rapid social and economic change, we have no choice but to latch onto ceaseless pronouncements and assertions that bear little if any relation to processes of critical thought and reflection.

It is possible that a quite novel situation thus afflicts us, one in which the ends of media representation also serve as the means by which the salient stories are told. If the medium represents a great deal more than the message, then analysis must turn to the technologies and their deployment, both new and enormously influential. Second, analysis must turn to the firms that wield such outsized power in the new digital environments. Third, analysis must also turn to what might be called the techniques of subjectification that impact anyone exposed to the forces of digital media influence today.

We know that savvy social media companies surveil clicks and likes to gather data on users and to build models and profiles of their online preferences. They feed these data through algorithms generated within self-referential systems usually inhabited by loosely like-minded people based upon aggregations of their web behavior. In this way, worlds are built, communities formed, commodities marketed and opinions articulated on the basis of repeated, steadily building invocations of what can be presented as discrete points of view. Of course, they never are. The degree of overlapping, repeated simulations is one of the most striking but least explored dimensions of the digital world's new political landscapes (Baudrillard 2002). So much for "all the news that's fit to print." Today's media environments are more like the rational-economic cultivation of systematic bias, breeding entities such as QAnon that traffic in falsehoods, misinformation and propaganda.

We, as the would-be critical public, are the poorer for it because one of the few open-access venues for public participation in opinion formation is now subject to powerful market forces that have a crippling impact on the quest for truth and integrity in reporting the facts. Worse still, those willing to play the game for mere attention and ratings are rewarded for outlandish behavior that incites and arouses on emotional registers and requires nary an investment of time and energy—and virtually no thought, just the ability to glance, click and scroll.

The skillful reversal of the process of social media opinion aggregation and mobilization was already evident back in July 2020, when teens utilized the messaging capacity of TikTok to flood the ticket distribution system for a Trump rally in Tulsa Oklahoma, leading event organizers to believe that demand for the gathering was in "the millions" and thus in need of an overflow venue to handle the expected crowd. When only 6,000 turned up, leaving an arena seating 16,000 more than half empty, Trump went on a rampage against his staff, returned home that night to the White House exhausted and dejected and soon fired his campaign coordinator.

Of course, such disruptive digital tactics as these by online activists are just a frittering away on the periphery of the media structure that has developed. They also raise serious questions in a democratic society about the protection of privacy. The ability of federal authorities to rely upon cellphone location data to tag the movements of rioters, for example, presents a serious risk to all citizens—as does the likelihood of the occasional case of mistaken identity through facial recognition technology applied on a mass scale.

Less fraught with issues of privacy and rights and far more effective as embodiments of media reform are the measures taken by the major media companies to patrol their own outlets and, in the case of Twitter and Facebook, to shut down accounts that are overtly focused on propagating misinformation. It would help, of course, if they explained these policies in terms that expressly endorsed such critical values as openness, democracy, constructive community building and the commitment to reason and science. Too often such measures get dragged into a misleading and crippling discourse about "censorship," "partisanship" or "cancel culture." The problem is, however, that from the standpoint of these media platforms the decision to shut down accounts selectively begins to compromise the larger commitment these firms have to running highly profitable businesses based upon the aggregation of data used to facilitate selectively targeted ad strategies.

If guidance is going to be found in this new media environment, it is more likely to be located among more traditional outlets that purport to produce and discuss the news and which have an inherent interest in the credibility of the product they offer, not to mention in the faith that consumers/readers/followers have in the integrity of that editorial product.

Considerable adjustment will be required for all of this to be widely adopted by the major media purveyors. On social media sites it will require closer scrutiny of posts deemed criminal or incendiary or in glaring contradiction to known truths. These corporate entities are not bound by the same First Amendment guarantees that federal and state governmental institutions are required to uphold. As providers of a service to customers engaged in a voluntary business enterprise in which users trade off participation and access for the likelihood of being subject to ads and solicitations, companies could simply be clearer about the terms of use and reserve the right to shut down posts or posters who violate their norms. Consumers, by contrast, would always have the choice of opting out of the platform if they believed the companies were practicing heavy-handed censorship. There would also always be the option of reverting to lesser-known alternative sites or to apps and the dark web of encryption and privacy where openness is more limited. That path, however, appears already to have been taken by right-wing networks in the aftermath of recent decisions by Facebook and Twitter to shut down openly incendiary users.

At the level of practice by journalists themselves there is much to be done, including pursuing the exemplary work of independent investigative researchers and organizations committed to democratic norms in their editorial work. In recent years journalists allied to major outlets have become celebrities themselves, with annual salaries at the network and cable outlets often reaching seven or eight figures for hosts, and regular guests who are interviewed as experts securing lucrative consulting contracts or benefitting from speaking fees, book contracts and widespread social media exposure. The lure of such rewards can be seductively distracting from the central task of creative journalism, which is to explore and tell a truthful, nuanced story while bringing perspective, depth and humanity to the subject—in the process empowering citizens by helping them to become more knowledgeable.

A viable independent alternative journalism is already taking form, slowly, and in a way that might well prove sustainable both as a business model and as a challenge to prevailing practice. The burden carried by conventional print media has always been cost of production and distribution. A printed issue requires reporters to write it, a production team to do the layout, a printer to convert it into a paper product, and a distribution network, usually through the postal system, or in the case of daily newspapers via personal delivery. This entails a laborious, costly process from inception to production and transportation, with time a factor as well. Internet journalism short circuits the entire process and makes it possible to write, edit, produce and distribute analysis in a virtually instantaneous and costless process. Thus, we see the proliferation of one-person operations flourishing these days, with Substack the preferred mode of delivery on the Internet on a regular/daily basis, with an optional subscriber window available that can easily generate enough revenue to make the effort worthwhile as fulltime work. Recognized journalists like Glenn Greenwald and Seth Abramson have found independent homes there, as has media critic Eric Boehlert with "Press Run." An otherwise reticent historian of nineteenth-century America, Heather Cox Richardson, converted her Facebook posts into a daily newsletter of a thousand words called "Letters from America," which has more than a quarter of a million readers, twenty thousand of whom are paying subscribers. The perspectives available on the likes of ad-free and algorithm-free outlets like Substack are far more critical and daring than those found in the mainstream media, and they provide a critical viewpoint for citizens seeking to be informed in an analytical way.

Understanding requires taking a step back. In the case of the news it means disengaging from the cacophonous immediacy of the latest breaking story or the most recent scandal involving some politician's verbal assault and exploring instead longer trajectories and deeper trends.

But trajectories and trends associated with what? That is where the politics becomes important. We need to think seriously—and self-critically—about the fate of originality, authenticity and autonomy in the context of these new developments.

Bibliography

Baudrillard, J. (2002) *Jean Baudrillard: Selected Writings*, Palo Alto: Stanford University Press.
Benjamin, W. (2019) *Illuminations: Essays and Reflections*, New York: Mariner Books.
Burgess, M. Commentary, *Wired*, 8 January 2020.
Gessen, M. (2020) *Surviving Autocracy*, New York: Riverhead Books.
Kendzior, S. (2020) *Hiding in Plain Sight: The Invention of Donald Trump and the Erosion of America*, New York: Flatiron Books.
LeBon, G. (1896) *The Crowd: A Study of the Popular Mind*, London: T. Fisher Unwin.
McGinniss, J. (1969) *The Selling of the President*, New York: Simon and Schuster.

4
THE ELUSIVENESS OF FASCISM

In the summer of 2020, during street protests in Portland, Oregon, that saw Department of Homeland Security officers, U.S. Marshals Service officers and Customs and Border Protection agents out in force conducting what appeared to be random arrests, a number of news analysts and commentators posed a question in op-ed pieces across the country: Is it time to call it fascism? What resulted was a strange political demurral, one that was virtually consensual in its denial given the ways in which rights were still widely assumed to be secure in America's liberal, constitutional order. Several features of the authoritarian ideology certainly stood out, noted the commentators, but it was too soon, or too undeveloped a situation, to warrant the label of "fascist."

Three-and-a-half years into the Trump presidency, propaganda laced with unusual viciousness was so widespread that it no longer seemed remarkable. By the summer of 2020 so-called post-facts politics was the hallmark of a considerable tranche of American political discourse. Far-right groups like QAnon and Proud Boys were active on social media, stirring hate-filled idolatry. Donald Trump's own displays of power took ominous forms, and he was anything but self-conscious about the bearing of a would-be authoritarian. He courted authoritarians in other countries, including Putin in Russia, Bolsonaro in Brazil, Erdoğan in Turkey, Duterte in the Philippines and North Korea's Kim Jong-un. A ruthless policy of cracking down on immigration by separating families at the border and holding hundreds of children apart from their parents remained firmly in place. Peaceful civil rights protests and gatherings intended to dissent against arbitrary police violence perpetrated on the Black community in cities across the United States were met with overwhelming police force, and communities of color experienced repression that bordered on paramilitary occupation. The rights of the LGBTQ communities were being officially withdrawn in the military and in the workplace.

The media were under withering attack by the president and his White House staff, with some news outlets and journalists singled out by name for their daring to challenge Trump at briefings and in their own editorials and news accounts. In the face of these erosions of basic liberties and traditions, Republican lawmakers maintained their steady silence and many even affirmed Trump's tactics—which at this point seemed like sport—and ceded to his inaction and consistent malfeasance when it came to the coronavirus pandemic. Yet, for commentators in the summer of 2020 it was not yet fascism—or so many voices seemed to agree. Fascism required something more: the seizure of the institutions of power by a single regime of governing authority, the censure of opponents backed up by an S.S.-like military police that invaded homes, seized property, imprisoned arbitrarily and the like. The United States had not reached that stage.

But for many of these commentators, fascism was defined in all-too-narrow political terms. It represented the political ascendance of a one-party regime that not only threatened to imperil the institutions of governance, but actually broke the institutions apart, installing new governing institutions in their place. Short of a *coup d'état*, fascism remained off the table.

In early June 2020 *Washington Post* columnist Ishaan Tharoor noted in an op-ed that even most scholars were loath to use fascism as a label for Trump, not to mention the Republicans who supported him. But many scholars did point to the "erosion underway during his presidency, the steady bending of norms and relentless attacks on those who don't show absolute loyalty to him, from political rivals to the free press." And, according to one historian, Federico Finchelstein, "We are still in a democracy and [Trump] cannot get away with it but he seems to be trying. … Fascists destroyed democracy from within and Trump so far is bastardizing democracy" (*Washington Post*, June 3, 2020).

But, in April and May of 2020, with dramatic police and private militias out in force in several American cities, most notably at the state capitol in Lansing, Michigan, the reluctance to label Trump's Administration fascist finally began to shift. In the *New York Times* Michelle Goldberg turned to historian Timothy Snyder for perspective. She invoked words Snyder used in his 2017 book, *On Tyranny*: "Be wary of paramilitaries. When the pro-leader paramilitary and the police intermingle, the end has come" (July 20, 2020). The end being that of liberal democracy.

More recently, in a *New York Times* op-ed, Paul Krugman argued that by early 2021, things had in fact changed—the time had come to call Trumpism for what it had become: fascist. "Trump is indeed a fascist—an authoritarian willing to use violence to achieve his racial nationalist goals. So are many of his supporters." Krugman went on to urge against appeasement, "which only emboldens fascists" (*New York Times*, January 7, 2021).

Following the far-right assault on the U.S. Capitol on January 6, 2021, Snyder explained in a lengthy *New York Times* analysis that Trump's lies ranged in size from small to medium to large. The large ones were what really counted, Snyder argued, and when Trump crossed the Rubicon in November of 2020 by asserting that he had won an election that he had in fact lost, Snyder suggested that the political landscape had dramatically shifted. The significance of this big lie, Snyder noted,

> resides in its demand that many other things must be believed or disbelieved. To makes sense of a world in which the 2020 presidential election was stolen requires distrust of not only reporters and experts, but also of local, state and federal government institutions, from poll workers to elected officials, Homeland Security and all the way to the Supreme Court. It brings with it, of necessity, a conspiracy theory: imagine all the people who must have been in on such a plot and all the people who would have had to work on the cover-up.
>
> *(New York Times, January 9, 2021)*

Snyder was right to point out that Trump's lies are likely to live on thanks to their endorsement by so many Republican members of Congress, as well as by other elected officials in many states. A further ominous suggestion was now part of the political reality, Snyder noted: far-right extremists now needed Trump to move to the background. At this point the right needed a political myth much larger than Trump, one that could ground itself in the conjuring of the imagined conception of the nation.

Before he uttered his Big Lie that the election results were fraudulent, Trump was, according to Snyder, something of a "pre-fascist." The "big lie is big, fundamentally, because it reverses the moral field of American politics and the basic structure of American history." The move to full-fledged fascism, Snyder suggested, would have been found in a strategy that Trump himself could not actually manage to bring about: he could not bring the nation's institutions to heel, and this was because neither Trump nor his supporters could articulate a vision of what their politics would ultimately amount to—what the Republican Party actually aspired to *do*. As Snyder wrote, referring to the January 6 insurrection, "It is hard to think of a comparable insurrectionary moment, when a building of great significance was seized, that involved so much milling around" (*New York Times*, January 9, 2021).

Milling around there was. But five people lost their lives, dozens of police officers and security personnel were assaulted, and significant destruction of federal property in the Capitol took place. And not least, there was a formidable show of menacing force by the hundreds who stormed the halls of government, many of them brandishing weapons and making dozens of Congresspersons (and most likely, a vice president) fearful for the widespread violence that could have ensued.

If it amounted to fascism, what *is* this fascism, exactly, and why should it be so concerning to Americans, if not the world? What is it that we do not properly understand about this relatively new political dynamic—new in terms of its emergence in the late nineteenth century (mainly in writing), and its deployment in the 1920s and 1930s?

We might begin by recalling that the ancient Greeks understood very well what demagoguery was, and they warned that it was an especially pernicious and ever-present danger in politics under the right conditions. But fascism is more than demagoguery. It is a uniquely late-modern dynamic, introducing altogether new qualities to an emerging political alchemy of rapidly modernizing societies. Historians of fascism point to the significance, for instance, of class, of loneliness in large industrial societies, of technology (the radio, TV, the Internet, social media), and of tensions arising from rural versus urban divides. Each of these elements appears to combine to give accelerants to wholly new political qualities—the charisma of an anointed leader, to be sure, but more importantly a submissive citizenry, one that was hypnotized and proved susceptible to dynamics of power that made the syndrome somewhat anti-political, decidedly anti-historical, and zealous in the assertion of a will-to-power that glorified violence and esteemed the authoritarian impulses that were transmitted by the leader to docile and subjugated masses.

Addressing these lesser-known qualities and dynamics requires analysis that is at once historical, theoretical and, most of all, political. In terms of historical experiences, we have models of fascism against which to measure what appears to be critical code required for Trump's governing logic. The rise of Mussolini in Italy in the early 1920s and the quixotic emergence of Hitler in Germany in the early 1930s both remain important benchmarks to consider. They take us to the heart of a series of interpenetrating dynamics that constitute fascism's most common, and most enduring, ingredients: war, economic dislocation, an isolated person in the context of societies speeding up, a frustrated middle class, a propensity toward violence in place of politics, and a uniquely positioned individual (Trump) shameless enough to seize and hold power without publicly having reservations about the consequences of his actions.

Of course, on the face of it, America today has little in common with Italy in the 1920s or with Germany in the 1930s. Both countries had only recently been stitched together from dozens of small principalities and republics, none of which enjoyed a strong democratic tradition. In both cases the urban industrial class was well organized and radicalized, while the rural sectors were left well behind in terms of organization, technology, education and civic participation. Church institutions remained firmly in place as political forces. Civic participation by the populace was extremely limited, as was a tradition of an independent press. In both countries, mass mobilization via democratic engagement was started up as an outlet for public discontent, and in both cases that mobilization generated significant pushback in the form of organized corporate enterprise aligning with a deeply entrenched military to quell unrest. Without that political organization—in the form of parliamentary party politics and labor radicalization—there would have been no consequent militarized response by the agents of nationalist reaction: police, army and private security.

Beyond these characteristics of the classic European fascist regime, today's popular discussion of authoritarianism in the United States has tended to focus on the play of personalities and the support they generate—on Trump and his personality and how far the Republican Party or Trump's base of supporters are willing to abide his tactics. This is largely obscured and thereby legitimated by the familiar "horse race" coverage of American politics. Here the sources of major policy differences and sentiments among sectors of the populace are subordinated to the superficiality of contemporary media discourse, one that mainly looks at candidates vying for votes or the way in which two parties, constructed as similar and mirroring each other, are arrayed across an aisle. But the problem is that this relative gamesmanship of partisan affection and "public opinion" overlooks the underlying structural nature of policy positions and interests, and at the same time the (potential) affinities this country demonstrates for a fascist breakthrough by those forces in civil society and economy that would most stand to benefit from it.

This takes us to one discomfiting reality of liberal democratic politics: fascism is ultimately inconceivable without democracy. The energies and unique inflection points of fascism's power require a broad base of support, one that draws people out of their isolation, their relative anonymity and frustration, and presents them with an aura of power that stands out against so many simulations, the multitude of copies in a world where abject superficiality and artificiality lull one into a state of somnambulism. The attraction of actual power is that it appears quite capable of changing the world. Lacking the confidence to secure an identity through the long hard haul of political activity, the temptation is strong to grab for an archaic symbol of previous greatness emblazoned on a badge or flag. It also helps the feeling of instant empowerment and the frustration with day-to-day norms of civility to grab a weapon and to ensure that the assertion of one's will does not get bogged down in the niceties and procedures of civic discourse or legislative procedure. Lacking a modicum of consensus on values with which to create governance through hegemony, the fascist seeks to create the basis for conformity of belief by the threat of force or by overt violence itself. Rather than relying upon the cultivation of shared values in what might be considered a more organic, peaceful, civic form, "unfathomable drives," in the words of Umberto Eco, are unleashed in an aspirational orgy of the real as well as the symbolic (Eco 1995).

This version of mass politics, in which rabid nationalism takes up slogans and presents itself as populism, traffics in lies, engages in conspiratorial shorthand, elicits militant patriotism, induces retro flag wielding and displays of arms—all of this is devoid of a self-critical, reflective political mentality. Such a mentality would invite the individual to act spontaneously as a responsible agent in concert with others, and on the basis of which the unity of humankind is affirmed. The fascist mentality leads to action which takes place in a democratic framework, but it is the opposite of inclusionary. It constitutes identity in a reductive, terrestrial, corporeal way that explicitly repudiates aspirational potential in classical political terms. It reads character off of a surface that is immutably locked into a mythic past, one that cannot be confronted or overcome or negotiated away. Presence is affirmed through the symbolic presentation of self rather than through a core identity of values that are acquired, learned, overcome or creatively articulated. In this sense, fascism mistrusts those who, through their speech acts, their learning, their creativity and imagination can foresee an alternative presence. Those realms are seen as threatening and have to be closed off.

Hence, fascism's attitudes toward the kinds of values normally associated with democratic politics. Fascism is not only anti-politics, it is anti-science, anti-art, anti-complexity and anti-uncertainty. By its very nature it must also be homophobic. Its attempt to ground itself in a mythological conception of homeland and nature also orients it toward anti-Semitism and anti-globalism. Its nativism and sense of racial superiority also make it an exemplar of rabid white supremacy. Racism has particular resonance in a country where the dominant white population faces a demographic decline and with it a loss of status. And yet fascism arises in a democratic context—or, to be precise, out of the inability of certain democratic practices to provide for the reward structures necessary to sustain the commitment of a citizenry to the laboring processes that ultimately comprise civil society. Civil society is seen as weak and inauthentic, a bastard version of the real, virile thing.

A further problem is evident as well, one that requires careful consideration at this particular historical juncture. It turns out that fascism is one of several alternatives to the difficulties that a system like liberal capitalism has in delivering, as promised, to its citizenry. In this century, as capitalist democracy has matured in terms of its reach into more and more areas of the market, and as it has absorbed more of the citizenry (importantly, wage workers and lower and middle-class consumers), it has often stumbled—badly—through cyclic overproduction, underconsumption, unemployment, inflation, depression and growing inequality between the owning classes and the productive classes. Karl Marx foresaw this structural issue in the early stages of industrial capitalism and assumed that the growing immiseration of a burgeoning sector of the populace—the working class—would generate enough pressure at the point of production to lead to a radical takeover of the "means of production" and, with it, distributive equality. As we now know from the history of nineteenth- and early twentieth-century capitalism, this analysis seriously overestimated the automatic nature of the workers' collective awareness and conviction. Marx also seriously underestimated the mechanisms of legitimation by which the cultural order of liberal democracy sustains itself by circulating through civil society an array of potential rewards, whether of a material, emotional or value-oriented sort, if not in the immediate future, then in a more distant one. These promises of rewards might pertain to wages, consumer durables constituting "the good life," emotional fulfillment, job satisfaction, the promise of the American Dream or at least leaving one's kids better off financially and educationally than one had it during one's own lifetime.

These cultural goods operate to placate discontent or at least to offset and delay its overt manifestations. And they are invariably accompanied by certain levers of centralized state management by which market relations are variously planned, coordinated and regulated to elicit a range of desired outcomes, whether to preserve the market system as a whole or to absorb some of its more crucial functions—heath care, utilities, education, housing—which, absent such management, would leave people defenseless against the ravages of the market.

Fascism is actually an obvious alternative to two other more activist methods by which liberal capitalism saves itself from dysfunction. It is the alternative to a liberal political intervention that substantially revises capitalism through shoring up savings, protecting workers rights, providing unemployment insurance, creating baseline support of the elderly and retired who might not otherwise have any savings, stabilizing currency, enacting price supports for agricultural goods that normally fluctuate wildly on world markets, and engaging in counter-cyclical spending to offset slack demand and unemployment, even if that means considerable deficit spending for extended periods of time. Second, it is the alternative to socialism, or social democracy, whereby state managers, working in conjunction with publicly sanctioned labor unions, coordinate management of production, supply and distribution in a variety of fields deemed essential to human dignity (transportation, education, health care, telecommunications and other basic utilities), with the state acting in effect as majority stock holder, while preserving a considerable share of the economy to privately owned market relations.

Either of these two alternatives presents a carefully worked out program that addresses the tensions between democracy and capitalism. Fascism, by contrast, turns its back on a market economy in crisis and dispenses with metrics oriented towards equity and redistributive justice. Its concern is less with the ability of the economy to deliver goods and services that people need, and more with preserving the existing system of property relations, regardless of the consequences for efficiency, utility or some measure of equality. It does so through a curious alliance of big business, the lower and middle classes, and rural peasantry/farmers.

Consequently, as a political formation fascism presents itself in ways that are difficult to capture fully. Students of political science have certainly tried to describe its essence, though in doing so they focus more on its overt manifestations (such as the glorification of violence, or the *führer* cult) than on its underlying ethic or dispositional roots. To be sure, fascism promotes the violent rejection of humanitarian ideals. It also prioritizes the *inevitability* of hierarchy, discipline and obedience, finding them to be values in and of themselves. Fascism thus invests solidarity in subservience. And fascism advocates violence by linking its necessity to some imperiled dimension of the polity, usually a race or a national claim that is capable of being wheeled out and worshipped. These dimensions are well known, and they are discussed in a great many textbooks and studies of European experiences during the interwar period.

Less well known are the longstanding sources of power that fuel the social and cultural orientations that foster the political outcome of fascism. The reluctance of commentators and analysts to identify Trump and far-right activists as fascists may reflect the fact that too often pride of place is given to the political outbursts of fascism, when it is the undercurrents—social, cultural and quasi-religious—that we should be examining. As we argue, fascism should be seen not as a state but as a continuum. Democracy, for that matter, must also be conceived not as a settled set of conditions, but as a fluid energy stream that consolidates and then recedes over time (Wolin 2016). Above all else, fascism is the culmination of social forces that create a dangerously unstable political admixture.

This instability means there is a weakness that anti-fascist politics can exploit. We discuss this in the conclusion, where we explore some possible remedies to the current condition. The point we want to make here is that fascism is usually assessed in terms of organizational capacities rather than as psychological and social-psychological dispositions. The latter are far more concerning, for they are unusually episodic and fluid and can morph quickly like some tactically nimble and strategically agile shape-shifting force that is difficult to pin down and thus to track in its development over time and across social and political space.

If ever there was a political concept stringently resistant to definition, it is fascism. The late Italian philosopher and semiotician Umberto Eco had it about right when he said that fascism enjoys "no quintessence." It is a "*fuzzy* totalitarianism, a collage of different philosophical and political ideas, a beehive of contradictions," a matter of "political and ideological discombobulation" (Eco 1995). So many of the defining features of fascism contradict one another. Hatred of governing elites is channeled as the worship of new elites is esteemed. Fascism requires democracy while fascists endeavor to obstruct the individual from participating in the political process. Fascism is *syncretistic*—it reflects the combination of contending elements and is especially adept at tolerating contradictions, even using them to its advantage. It rails against conspiracies, which it sees everywhere; then has to constitute itself as such in order to advance its various plays for power beyond the reach of accountability. Unlike any other political ideology, fascism is an especially mobile apparatus of dispositions, an unusually adaptable structure of social relations and cultural undercurrents. In the right conditions, fascist leaders derive a great deal of their power from this essential fact.

Both Hitler and Mussolini proved especially adept at summoning the will of the masses when it suited an urgent political necessity. But as the biographer of Hitler, Ian Kershaw, has observed, Hitler—who enjoyed the more air-tight ideology of the two—exhibited a curious dependence upon the political imagination of the masses and their anticipation that whatever abuse of power the masses were inclined to accept was one that the *führer* himself would in fact have counseled. The fascist leader exploits a terribly ambiguous gray area between ruler and ruled (Kershaw 1993: 113–117). The leader is simply not all-powerful. He relies on the anxiousness of the masses to underwrite what they understand to be the inevitability of his authority structure, and this involves a terrific leap of faith. The socio-cultural circumstances are so fluid that an anything-goes approach to politics will usually be rewarded. Time will be stopped, for a period of time. Truth and meaning can be assigned, at least for a time, until the next iteration of confusion and inanity obtains, thereby demanding another assertion of will—of what can be made to count as the necessity of action in a specific situation. Witness Trump's weekly assertions of X being X, the next day that X is actually Y, and the following day that neither X nor Y are at issue. The people would be left dumbfounded if they were not in the thrall of a political tactician acting like a magician.

Thus, while it is customary to characterize fascism as an ideology, there is considerable evidence to suggest that fascism transcends that category, introducing as it does dynamics that are religious and psycho-social and are therefore unstable and unseeable. Of course, there are ideological aspects embedded in a fascist politics. Ideas that are assumed to have some level of fundamental relation to the past, present and the future are invoked and leveraged in the name of a cause that aspires to total control of the population and the illegitimate authority of the levers of state of power. But fascists are not inclined to put forth what is usually necessary for ideological affirmation. There is no vision of a world beyond the arbitrary play of hierarchical power and use of violence to ensure subservience to (what is usually) a single leader's own political proclamations.

Nevertheless, some of the more astute theorists of fascism, among them Karl Polanyi and Franz Neumann, point to several common broad dynamics. First among them is the failure of the capitalist market system to serve people's basic interests. Fascist leaders appealed to frustrated middle class expectations, and they found strong support in rural areas, in particular among small landholders.

Second, fascism develops after democracy has failed and when institutional deadlock sets in. Fascism amounts to the entrance of the "masses" into politics—not as some collective of autonomous, self-critical agents, but in the agglomeration of disembodied political souls, of alienated, estranged individuals with scarcely any capacity for independent thought and analysis.

Third, fascism develops through the "spread of irrationalistic philosophies, racialist aesthetics, anticapitalist demagogy, heterodox currency views, criticism of the party system and widespread disparagement of the [existing] 'regime'" (Polanyi 2001: 246). One is reminded here of Trump's calls to "drain the swamp," presumably referring to a realm of professionals, experts and experienced decision makers whose disinterested engagement according to law and rational guidelines cannot be trusted because it is based upon abstract principles instead of self-interest. Perhaps it is just an empty phrase. More likely, it is a shorthand for distrust of those who work by rules, science and public interest. In any case, the person elected to empty the presumed detritus promptly creates an enormous morass filled at the cabinet and agency levels with the most corrupt assemblage of grifters ever gathered to run a government—and he was promptly rewarded for it by nearly getting re-elected.

Fourth, fascism is a deflection of self-responsibility, a cover for the failure of agents to take actions for themselves. One requires a cover for the fact that one is not trying to contribute anything to improvement even within the most narrow of political limits. The responsibility of self-governance is shifted from self to others. Accountability disappears, and no one is responsible for the outcome who can be publicly identified. This reflects the build-up of negativity as a constant resource for agitation. The motive of negativity reflects the twin dynamic of desiring to make a commitment while avoiding the harder work of political affirmation. To affirm politically requires arduous and sustained effort. It also requires a higher degree of commitment. Vague criticism is a much easier lift, and it can be appropriated in a wide array of political locales to achieve the same outcome—distrust, obfuscation and paralysis, all in the absence of identifiable purpose. When combined with the anti-science, anti-intellectual and anti-truth orientations that underlie a fascist epistemology, the result is an inability to move in any constructive way, all while creating an image of turbulent engagement and coordinated action. Fascism only appears busy; it is actually the lazy way out.

Political theorists who have studied fascist cultures frequently point to the significance of loneliness, the forgotten person of the masses who now—as a result of a pseudo political awakening—aspires to some kind of agency, desires to "be someone," and acquires an identity rooted not in the transience of social life, but in a more durable political movement. The term *movement*, however, is used advisedly. Polanyi observed that fascism was an "ever-given political possibility, an almost instantaneous emotional reaction in every industrial community since the 1930s" (Polanyi 2001: 247). He called it a "move" rather than a "movement" because the crisis with which it was associated was so impersonal, the symptoms being "vague and ambiguous." At the time, in the 1930s, few accepted criteria of fascism existed. It amounted to an amorphous social force that waxed and waned according to the situation at hand in one beleaguered country after another.

It was this situation that Frankfurt School scholars endeavored to understand out of the mass of data they accumulated on public opinion after the Second World War. Their term for what they examined was "social totality." This term meant the broad social interrelations experienced by a society, and they could include things like a "general malaise" about the entire social condition. Peoples' views on the general social conditions may not be rational as such, and thus they are difficult to ascertain, but they form the basis of a sociopsychological situation that can nonetheless be harnessed as a powerful social force (Adorno et al. 2019). Just because a variable is hard to operationalize behaviorally or quantitatively does not render it irrelevant. Indeed, it may tell us more about the explanatory limits of a certain kind of social science than it does about the stubborn elements underlying fascism.

Umberto Eco, certainly not a social scientist in the strict sense, ventured as many as fourteen defining characteristics of fascism, among them a cult of tradition, the rejection of modernity, irrationalism, fear of difference, middle-class frustration, nationalism, popular elitism and selective populism. Fascism's fluidity consigned it to a great number of likely fellow travelers: fear and loneliness, estrangement and isolation, outsider and insider, nationalist and zealot, and so forth. What mattered most was what many observers and analysts of the 1930s described as an atmosphere, a climate, that manifested as a toxic mixture of social ebullience and trepidation. The masses were disposed to act, up on their toes and itching for a fight against whatever foe could be presented as a deserving enemy. Arrogance combined with mysticism and the political residue of the occult. "Where the arrogance of intellect mates with spiritual antiquatedness, and bondage, there the Devil is," wrote Thomas Mann in 1929 (cited in Kurzke 2002: 484).

Fascism, perhaps more than any other political concept, demands a level of skill with political thinking that surpasses most people, certainly most Americans, and most of all, *young* Americans. Notoriously so difficult to define, the idea is thus largely avoided. When it is taken up in discussions about nascent political developments, one notes a certain nervousness when the term is deployed, as if a disruptive element has been introduced that no one quite knows how to handle. One does not want to appear a flat-footed ideologue, pronouncing willy-nilly something that is so beyond the pale of civil discourse or the normal boundaries of a three-minute TV conversation among guest analysts. Introducing the term seems so irremediably *bad*, by nature so *evil*, that one is embarrassed to appear so scandalous wielding a complex concept with such odious moral and political weight and historical baggage.

Perhaps that explains why, until fairly recently, a good many commentators rejected the term's appropriateness and value relative to describing the Trump Administration. But perhaps there is another reason fascism remains so mystifying for us. Fascism, after all, is also to be understood as what it is not. Fascism, as we have emphasized, is an uneven process more than it is a settled state. It reflects a perpetual insecurity of its own lack of a stable ground upon which to consolidate some political program. Ian Kershaw's portrait of Hitler is again instructive: the charismatic leadership model that Hitler succeeded in building

> fits a form of domination which could never settle down into "normality" or routine, [or] draw a line under its achievements and come to rest as conservative authoritarianism, but was compelled instead to sustain the dynamism and to push ceaselessly and relentlessly for new attainments in the quest to fulfill its chimeric goal.
>
> *(Kershaw 1993: 118)*

What was that goal? Hitler's broad aim was the restoration of German glory— "make Germany great again," one might say—in large part through establishment of a racial nation. But the goal was not nearly as important as the constant agitation that defers the realization of a political program.

> In its struggle for political power fascism is entirely free to disregard or to use local issues, at will.... Its aims transcend the political and economic framework. ... It puts a political religion in the service of a degenerative process.
>
> *(Polanyi 2001: 249)*

Even today there is growing acknowledgement that fascism is a political alternative developed out of a series of tensions between the free-market economy and democracy. It should therefore be no surprise that socialism figured prominently in the minds of populists organized under Trumpism. It provided, for example, the shorthand for a campaign against the two Georgia Democrats, Rev. Raphael Warnock and Jon Ossoff, who challenged the two incumbent Republican senators during the runoff election on January 5, 2021. The calumny of "socialism" quickly became part of the carefully calibrated messaging by which Republicans on Capitol Hill joined the Trump base outside Washington, DC, in trying to fend off what they perceived as a left-wing takeover by incoming President Biden, a takeover that was being secretly engineered by Senator Bernie Sanders and Congressperson Alexandria Ocasio-Cortez. The Red-baiting is a giveaway of the need to define oneself, not only in opposition but in a way that justifies a whole world view animated by one's own turbulent, volatile mix of anger, resentment and rage.

Perhaps after the events of January 6, 2021, it will be easier to identify fascism when it arises. The images that emerged of the protesters at the Capitol and of those who assaulted the Capitol building itself reveal something striking: the number of cellphones being wielded, ostensibly for purposes of photographing the moment. What does the function of the cellphone mean in this context? What might the protesters and insurrectionists have been doing had they not had their cellphones at hand? The use of these devices betrays a condition of social and political isolation and of the desire to overcome that anomie in a moment of profound violence. What mattered were not just the connections being forged with those immediately around the grounds, but the transmitting of photographic signs to a virtual community of fellow co-conspirators with whom assailants were in one-way communication.

There is a final concern to register here. Evidence suggests that the fascist syndrome changes people at a fundamental level, and there is evidence also that it can do so with breathtaking speed. The political philosopher Leszek Kolakowski has noted that authoritarianism introduces a political dynamic that activates and enables a morally depleted psychology of hatred, one that is ultimately capable of destroying the person. Moral helplessness ensues. In fact, authoritarians are forced to educate people to hate: "Hatred's pure negativity, which paralyzes all human communication, also destroys the inner unity of personality, and hence it is irreplaceable as a means to disarm the human soul" (Kolakowski 1997: 258).

Such connections between the inner psychology of hatred and the resulting fascist political manifestation deserve much greater attention by social scientists. But doing so will require dispensing with familiar analytical categories that separate out politics and culture, social dimensions of power from political and economic dimensions and religious dimensions from all of the above. Integrated perspectives need to develop filiations among all of these areas of human feeling and action, and they must be infused with an historical and theoretical sensibility that can critically explore hidden areas of power, both good and bad.

This, of course, is a tall order. It takes a tremendous amount of work to educate citizens to resist the powerful pull of believing even more intensely what they already believe, or what others around them believe, or what would make sense given their own previous choices.

Herein lies an important fact about our political moment. Peoples' past decisions are difficult for most to disavow. A willingness to look at oneself in the mirror requires that we have access to mirrors and a willingness to confront the fact that we can make mistakes. It must be said that the cellphone, and just about the entirety of social media, are instruments of obfuscation and diversion from the real concerns of our time. Over seventy million Americans voted for a second term for Donald Trump. That is an astonishing number, and it suggests, if nothing else, that the fascist syndrome is only just beginning. Its reversal will take years. In the next chapter we offer an analysis of how that syndrome inculcated itself in American political culture and how it can be combatted.

Bibliography

Adorno, T.W. et al. (2019) *The Authoritarian Personality*, London: Verso.
Eco, U. (1995) "Ur-Fascism," *The New York Review of Books*, 22 June. www.nybooks.com/articles/1995/06/22/ur-fascism/
Kershaw, I. (1993) "Working Towards the Führer: Reflections on the Nature of the Hitler Dictatorship," *Contemporary European History* 2(2), pp. 103–118.
Kolakowski, L. (1997) *Modernity on Endless Trial,* Chicago: University of Chicago Press.
Kurzke, H. (2002) *Thomas Mann: Life as a Work of Art,* Princeton: Princeton University Press.
Polanyi, K. (2001) *The Great Transformation: The Political and Economic Origins of Our Time,* Boston: Beacon Press.
Snyder, T. (2017) *On Tyranny: Twenty Lessons from the Twentieth Century*, New York: Crown.
Wolin, S.S. (2016) *Fugitive Democracy and Other Essays*, Princeton: Princeton University Press.

5
SOCIAL DEMOCRACY

Any public discussion that takes seriously the very real possibility of fascism necessarily entails an account of the prospects for resistance as well as alternative cultural and governing arrangements. Social democracy is one such alternative. We will be hearing much more about it in the coming years, though most of what we will be subjected to will be distortion and dismissal based upon customarily reactionary responses of "Red-baiting." Americans would do well to pay attention to serious engagements with the concept. In this chapter we offer a primer, one focused not on economic policy management but on the spirit of social democracy and its importance in the contemporary context.

We are not concerned to examine or even briefly rehearse the ideological origins and offshoots associated with social democracy and socialism. Instead, we explore aspects of a politics that constitute something of an *affect* or *disposition* of everyday life, a disposition that is linked to the meaning of being a citizen and a political being. Fascism and authoritarianism, after all, are animated by distinctive emotional sensibilities, many of them based upon thoughtlessness, cruelty, mean-spirited reaction, and a culture that makes a sport of dehumanization. Social democracy, as we show, radiates a political spirit around the virtues of openness, inclusiveness and empathy. An ethos grounded in what are essentially democratic virtues deserves some elaboration if a case is to be made for a renewed understanding of citizenship and democracy in a post-pandemic era.

Socialism is commonly associated with an oppositional economic vision to that supplied by free-market capitalism. Consequently, it usually points toward an anti-capitalist or post-capitalist economy that claims to better serve the people. As a political concept social democracy travels in close quarters with socialism, and it is often presented as offering an alternative vision to political liberalism. Such liberal associations reflect a prioritizing of economic

DOI: 10.4324/9781003268741-6

over political relationships and thus are quite limiting, especially given the predicaments that concerned us in the previous chapters. Our objective here is to emphasize political aspects of social democracy while not downplaying important dimensions of the capitalist economy that should be under discussion; a whole host of economic realities are obviously important to consider at this historical juncture. But it is the politics of a social democratic vision that deserves greater attention amidst the social and cultural pressures and incentive structures we see in the United States today.

To anticipate this vision, it may help to pose some questions that describe dimensions of public life that we have argued are too easily closed off in the cacophony of narrow partisan debate and constant media noise. What are the character traits embedded in social and political experiences represented by the ongoing struggle for civil rights? What are the everyday life experiences associated with the sense of a shared political purpose, with "the sense of reality," to invoke remarks James Baldwin made in 1965, faced by people who cannot participate in the public or private spheres where the more affluent exercise power (Baldwin 1965)? What is the sense of reality enjoyed by the privileged? Is there a spirit of shared identity that can stand up to the sectarian pronouncements of affluence and privilege, especially those animated by cruelty and vengeance? What does it feel like to be linked to other people in a national context without relying upon aggressive strategies of mobilization like militarization, or being aroused by the sentiments embodied in xenophobia and even patriotism? If experiences of shared purpose are real, what does it feel like to achieve their realization even if those experiences are momentary, all-too-fleeting recognitions of shared interests and common political projects? What is the meaning of those moments when you engage others in a public setting to esteem the obligations of citizenship—by getting vaccinated, voting, paying taxes, and donning a mask in public space? How can these feelings be honored as the embodiment of the duty to others that necessarily obtains among citizens as well as non-citizen residents of any democratic polity? If we catch glimpses of these moments and actions, are there ways in which citizens might build more of them into everyday experiences of national life? What would it mean, politically, to do so?

In this chapter we eschew the task of reconstructing the long, rich history of socialism. Many good guides are available for this task, including John Judis's recent *The Socialist Awakening* (2020). Tony Judt's *Ill Fares the Land* (2011) remains a valuable resource, as well. Americans would do well to consult resources both old and new, if only for a better understanding of a political tradition that electorates in many of the world's major democracies enthusiastically embrace. Indeed, one of our aims is to expand Americans' understanding of the economic and political developments that have forced societies—advanced societies in particular—to develop greater governing capacities and, ultimately, strategies geared toward the legitimate uses of authority and power in those spheres of governance bearing on the entire province of the democratic landscape.

A related task is to elaborate a conception of social democracy that can better inform Left political thinking and action in the United States at the present moment. Our premise is a belief that economic and social policymaking in the United States will be forced to move much further to the Left than it has at any other time in the past several generations. By "the Left" we mean in the direction of social justice, racial and environmental rectitude, and government planning relative to the direction of the economy and especially in terms of the impact of the economy on the country's ability to serve the interests of the least advantaged.

But there is a rub. If it is true that social democracy means subordinating the economy to democracy, then what does this subordination mean at a time when democracy has been so badly damaged—corrupted by special interests, corroded by degrading public trust, and compromised by crippled institutions that fail to operate? We consider this difficult question here and in the chapters that follow.

Just after 5 a.m. on February 5, 2021, after an intense all-night session, the U.S. Senate voted to move ahead—under an obscure budget resolution requiring only a "simple majority"—with a $1.9 trillion pandemic relief package, a comprehensive initiative designed to extend disaster relief to millions of struggling families, relieve the fiscal pressures faced by all 50 states, and curtail the deadly advance of the coronavirus. Newly sworn-in Vice President Kamala Harris cast the deciding vote on a bill supported by all 50 of the Senate's Democrats. Not one Republican Senator voted in favor of the resolution. Later that Friday in the House of Representatives the bill also saw approval, again along party lines—all Democrats supporting the legislation and not a single Republicans voting in favor. President Biden—the chief architect of the plan—signed the legislation before unemployment insurance was set to expire for many Americans in early March.

The bill extended support to local and state governments for COVID-19 testing and contact tracing as well as vaccine distribution. As of mid-2021, $400 billion of the relief package had been directed to the public health crisis, including funding a national vaccination program and providing paid sick leave to help contain the virus's spread. The plan included more than $1 trillion in direct aid to families and increased stimulus checks from $600 (contained in the December 2020 relief package) to somewhere between $1,400 and $2,000. It extended unemployment insurance, rental protection and nutrition assistance for many families. It also gave direct aid to businesses, much of it targeted—$440 billion to small businesses, local communities and transit systems (ensuring workers were kept on the payrolls and service cuts avoided). Another provision in the initial draft of the legislation that would have raised the minimum wage to $15 per hour did not receive enough support in the Senate for inclusion in the bill, but a generous child tax credit was extended for children in poor and middle-class households.

The bill was designed to be a relief package, not an economic stimulus. And it was massive—on the order of 10 percent of the nation's GDP. Comparisons were drawn to FDR's New Deal. In an op-ed in the *Washington Post* a day before the resolution's passage, the economist Lawrence Summers expressed caution about the proposed size of the spending package, which he said represented the "boldest act of macroeconomic stabilization in U.S. history." While tacitly endorsing a measure that erred on the side of being too big, Summers cited inflationary pressures as a risk that policymakers needed to take seriously. He also warned that the bill contained "essentially no increase in public investment to address … economic injustice, slow growth and inadequate public investment in infrastructure, pre-school education and renewable energy." Summers's larger message was drowned out by the word "risks" contained in the op-ed's headline. In words President Biden might have used, Summers urged lawmakers to take measures to "build back better through public investment," arguing the relief package represented just a beginning, not an end, to the country's larger fiscal predicament and the country's massive public investment shortfalls.

Early on in the presidency of Donald Trump the Republicans had rushed through Congress the Tax Cuts and Jobs Act of 2017. That bill reduced tax rates for businesses and individuals, increased the standard deduction and family tax credits, eliminated personal exemptions and canceled the penalty enforcing the individual mandate of the Affordable Care Act. The tax benefits of this legislation flowed disproportionately to the wealthy and to corporations. The Congressional Budget Office estimated that the legislation would ultimately add around $2.29 trillion to the national debt over the ensuing ten years. Again, there was a stark partisan divide—the bill received support from all Republicans, but no Democrats.

Separated by a mere three years, but framed by the greatest public health crisis in a century, these two pieces of legislation represent what is perhaps the most consequential divide in American politics today. We speak not of the gulf that separates the Left and the Right, but instead of the divisions sown by the Republican Party over some forty years, with policy priorities tacking harder to the right than many (including several leaders within the party) thought possible. To a significant degree, government power has been co-opted by well-financed and skillful strategists of the right who have managed to strip power from the Democrats. The party whose platform remains "the smaller the size of government, the better" has essentially expanded the size of government dramatically—through, among other things, spending on two major wars in the Middle East—and fought hard to maintain control over it. This happened to the great detriment of the country's immediate and long-term prospects for addressing major domestic challenges: from rising inequality, declining opportunities available to the young (and especially non-whites) and a carbon economy. Democrats advocate for public policy aimed at helping the least well off, generally, and are unafraid to plan for the future (from access to education, expanded health and elder care, infrastructure investment to energy policy). Nor are they shy about supporting state and local governments in a federal system that recognizes the autonomy of 50 states, each of which faced huge shortcomings during a national crisis in part as a result of this autonomy. The other side pursues an agenda that further concentrates wealth in the hands of the rich and powerful in the name of economic freedom and political liberty. Given the evidence, the Republicans' goals can only be regarded utopian. They are designed to divert attention from the stubborn reality of socio-economic inequalities, the toll of years of underinvestment in a vast array of public services and mounting social and environmental costs that will only compound long into the future if they remain unaddressed.

By the spring of 2021 there were signs that the coronavirus pandemic had finally pulled the Left and more moderate constituencies away from center- to right-leaning positions, most importantly the neoliberal position most Democrats occupied since the start of the Clinton Presidency in 1993. As early as April of 2020 a hint of that shift had arrived in the form of an editorial-board piece in the *Financial Times*. Surprisingly uncharacteristic for the British newspaper, the write-up declared that the coronavirus pandemic "has injected a sense of togetherness into polarized societies." Along with the economic lockdowns, the editorial went on, the pandemic shines

> a glaring light on existing inequalities—and even create[s] new ones. Beyond defeating the disease, the great test all countries will soon face is whether current feelings of common purpose will shape society after the crisis. As western leaders learnt in the Great Depression, and after the Second World War, to demand collective sacrifice you must offer a social contract that benefits everyone.
>
> *(Financial Times,* 3 April 2020*)*

This may have been an optimistic reading of the situation, but if reckoning there is, it is one that expresses not merely the growing recognition of precarity during a pandemic, but aims to issue a more substantial report on the colossal failures of public policy devolving from decades of neoliberal policies. The coronavirus may have *caused* the 2020–2021 economic crisis, but it also introduced a vital comeuppance for which Americans in particular were long overdue. What, after all, are economies *for*? Who do they principally *serve*? When time-honored economic truths no longer hold, *who pays*? What is owed to society's most vulnerable, the weakest and least able to help themselves—in "ordinary" times as well as during a crisis? The *Times* concluded,

> [c]ountries that have allowed the emergence of an irregular and precarious labour market are finding it particularly hard to channel financial help to workers with such insecure employment. Meanwhile, vast monetary loosening by central banks will help the asset-rich. Behind it all, underfunded public services are creaking under the burden of applying crisis policies … Radical reforms—reversing the prevailing policy direction of the last four decades—will need to be put on the table. Governments will have to accept a more active role in the economy. They must see public services as

investments rather than liabilities, and look for ways to make labour markets less insecure. Redistribution will again be on the agenda.

(Financial Times, 3 April 2020)

In America the neoliberal trend of steady divestment from public works projects has taken place over decades, but in recent years calls for a viable left-wing agenda have been quietly building. This development has been in part a reaction to a Republican shift to the right since Barack Obama was first elected president. It has also been aroused by the devastation wrought by a weakening social welfare system that comes nowhere close to meeting the needs of ordinary Americans. The withdrawal of services and loss of opportunities are now strikingly in evidence. Calls for a Left political vision were issued during the protests in opposition to the 2003 Iraq War, then under the banner of the Occupy Movement of 2008–2011, and most recently in opposition to the politics of Trump and the nationalism and xenophobia his presidency has so tragically reflected and shaped.

Yet, one must also consider a much wider frame of reference. The shift of the Republican Party to the far right has actually been happening gradually, if fitfully, since at least the early 1980s. From this perspective it is important to highlight five significant moments over a forty-year period that were decisive in terms of delivering us to the present predicament. First, the Clinton "moderate Left" politics that basically endorsed a version of Reagan's political and economic philosophy. Second, the election of G.W. Bush in 2000 and America's disastrous foreign policies after 9/11. Third, the rise of the Tea Party. Fourth, Mitch McConnell's Senate leadership during the Obama Presidency. And finally, the build-up of nativist xenophobia that intensified during the Obama presidency and which led to the election of Donald Trump in 2016. Using these moments as markers allows us to track developments that otherwise are difficult to follow as we assess missed opportunities as well as the major casualties in America's recent experiences with de-democratization (Brown 2017). What risks does America run today if the country cannot develop a formidable left-wing alternative to the Republicans' policies of tax reductions for the wealthy, regulatory rollbacks on corporations, and across-the-board public investment shortfalls?

By left-wing we mean planning for the long term through government policies that aim to protect and enhance the public interest. Reckoning with curtailed provisions that would have helped to ensure the public interest means that social policies today must inevitably contend with most citizens all but abandoning any conception of the meaning and purpose of a public life. An unintended effect is that rising inequality, widening social tensions and dangerous deferrals with respect to environmental rectitude will be greeted as so many inevitable developments necessarily associated with a political system that continues to reward elites and mainly serves government bureaucrats, those living on the coasts, or people with a favorable birthright. The democratic spirit further erodes as social dynamics—like racism, corruption, a culture of corporate malfeasance and predation, and most costly of all, a general lack of trust—take hold in the absence of progressive policies. Social programs are inescapably tasked with ensuring civil stewardship and bringing about a political ethos of generosity and mutual regard for all citizens of the national community.

Perhaps the most difficult challenge any community faces is the decision about who is deserving of "full membership," and thus in the American context the full set of rights enshrined in the Constitution—most importantly impartial treatment before the law. Democracy simply means that the people hold the power, but in its late-modern form it defers almost entirely on the question of who, exactly, "the people" are. In a time when politics is so severely warped by identity, democracies require a supplement through which discussions of inclusion and membership can take place. What this supplement amounts to is an historical sensibility not usually associated with the establishment and functioning of institutions. Democracy needs to be nurtured in order to ensure that shared power is not eroded over time, especially as new governing challenges arise (think of sovereign wealth funds and private equity groups, social media companies and AI) and as identities get shaped through such new developments.

Social and cultural life are unusually fluid these days, and the ways in which they constitute and effect political life must continually be looked after. In schools, in churches, in civic meetings, and in so many other spaces of citizens' lives, people must learn to acquire an understanding of a political quotient that Sheldon Wolin once referred to as "the presence of the past" (Wolin 1987). This means that people come to grasp, and constantly work to reflect upon, the purpose of the political community amidst new pressures that are applied on a collective life. An understanding of the value of holding things in common must be deliberately cultivated. This means rediscovering and rethinking the past on a continual basis. There is no better way to protect public life against the onslaught of new social forces and the worldviews they help to usher in.

Americans still appear not to appreciate how the virtues of social democracy can be used to infuse the political culture with a consciousness of the value of the entire political collective. As MAGA America struggles to consolidate identities on the basis of some mythical essence, we should take notice of aspects of American*ness* that are embedded in that imagined past, especially those that celebrate attributes of whiteness: from "real work ethics" or "real jobs" to the patriarchal family, resurgent masculinism, heteronormative dominance and Christianized communities.

The more interesting and historically appropriate questions bearing on identity are actually located not at the center, but at the margins, where distinctions between us and them are harder to make and nigh impossible to sustain over time. "Dreamers" represent identities at the edges of American life, as do recently arrived refugees from Afghanistan. What counts as the center is contested, of course, but lives at the margins of national identity represent a distinctive status. They are the *difference* against which the *identity* at the center strives to consolidate itself

(Connolly 1991). While the identity of MAGA America is largely fictive, it is more important to stress that it is dependent upon an emotional register that agitates to judge and condemn because of a feeling of precarity at the center. Pointing this out allows a conversation to begin about the ways in which a remarkable array of social and cultural characteristics—differences all—make up the political body. They strengthen and ennoble the polity—something that many smart, tolerant and forward-looking civilizations figured out long ago. Social democracy makes this a signature emblem in the polity's social and cultural fabric.

Even absent the pandemic and the economic crisis of 2020–2021, of late the risk assessment for America's turbulent experience with democracy points to the massive problem of widening income inequality. Yet, inasmuch as economic inequality may stand as the gravest threat to the country, more serious challenges are evident today, none of which can be decoupled from the reality of widening gaps between rich and poor. In important respects the consolidation of far-right power in America after Trump's win in 2016 was a result of structural forces that have been building since the early 1970s as the postwar consensus began to break down. Spending on Great Society programs and on the Vietnam War, working- and middle-class wage and income stagnation, unattainable post-secondary education, unequal access to healthcare, and—into the 1980s—terminations of pensions, abandonment of urban spaces and so on have all delivered the United States to a condition of political deadlock. The lack of citizens' trust in government and a surge of displays of hostilities toward one another have propelled the country to a condition that political theorists have long warned inevitably leads to some of the most dangerous social and political developments a nation can face. "If ever there was a political movement that responded to the needs of an objective situation and was not a result of fortuitous causes, it was fascism," observed Karl Polanyi in 1944 (Polanyi 2001: 245). It was during the height of the Second World War that Polanyi and other thinkers issued such warnings: fascism

> offered an escape from an institutional deadlock which was essentially alike in a large number of countries, and yet, if the remedy were tried, it would everywhere produce sickness unto death. That is the manner in which civilizations perish.
>
> *(245)*

As explained in the previous chapter, parallels to the interwar period bring to light tendencies that are hard to see in the moment. None of them makes headlines. When major economies refuse to work in cooperation through trade and investment; when monetary policy is chaotic; when unemployment or underemployment is high; and when factions emerge that exploit existing divisions which up to that time had not yet fractured along class, ethnic, racial and religious lines—when such conditions obtain, civil unrest and major diplomatic tensions can precipitate a turn to widescale violence, and eventually to war. All of these developments were linked to economic fundamentals, but the compounding of anxieties and animosities ultimately make the search for initial triggers and prime movers a fool's errand. The First World War was the culmination of many longstanding geopolitical developments—the end of empires, the shift to market economies, an inflexible exchange-rate system, and the entrance of new nation-states into the trading system (Australia and Argentina were the China and India of that time). Industry had become modern, but the political and cultural environments were incapable of adapting to the basic economic dynamics of the first great era of globalization, marked as it was by growing social disunity (Frieden 2020; Polanyi 2001: 231–244).

Today we are presented with structures of power of equal, and perhaps greater, significance. The present situation requires careful attention to what we would refer to as "developments in the making." Steel and agricultural products were the key staples of production and trade in the late nineteenth century, with steamships and railroads the new forms of transportation. Needless to say, the knowledge economies of today are vastly different. Digital communications technologies, the internet of things and artificial intelligence all conspire to alter radically dynamics of labor and will profoundly reshape the economies of the future. We are told that people's resistance comes from a growing sense of a lost world, where hands-on work was performed by people who labored together and lived in the same communities, worshipped at the same churches and attended the same schools (Hochschild 2018). Lived experiences in actual communities gave people the means for orienting their lives, and while wars and business cycles caused major interruptions, life—however tumultuous—was rooted in face-to-face interactions where peoples' sense of time was mostly consistent with previous generations' experiences. Peoples' expectations of a predictable future were dependent on good jobs, stable companies, and—after Medicare—a relatively comfortable if modest retirement. Much of that world, seemingly stable, now exists in a state of upheaval, and this has contributed to other social and cultural headwinds that stir animosities and stoke grievances with which social scientists are only now beginning to come to terms (Connolly 2019).

Analysts and media organizations must do their utmost to separate out cause and effect while also attending to the multiplying, compounding effects that generate great and seemingly intractable problems. Moreover, if the interwar period is any guide, an awful logic of ignorance and inaction resulting in widespread violence could also loom ahead. Americans have already seen how civil unrest can lead to paramilitary responses. Intensifying racism and anti-Semitism along with rising nationalism and pervasive jingoism (not limited to Fox News) could well become projected beyond our borders, provoking conflict abroad. In fact, one of the great surprises of the Trump Administration is that it did *not* deploy new military forces overseas as his willingness to foment social unrest and counsel widespread violence reached a crescendo in late 2019 and early 2020. Instead, he turned that violent animus inward against the country's own population.

In sum, huge challenges have emerged in the nation's politics over a long period of time. And they remain in spite of Joe Biden's election. Voter suppression initiatives are on the agendas of many state legislatures. The Senate filibuster is almost certain to remain in place, what essentially amounts to a vestigial institutional bulwark against progressive change. Dehumanizing anti-immigrant policies are still very much in force. Women's right to choose is being drastically cut back in many states. And we must also add to the classical volatile mixture of entrenched divisions among several constituencies (urban, rural, black and brown, white, the poor, and the aged) the introduction of digital (and especially social) media, the decline of print journalism and local news reporting, along with an array of viral transmission belts that spin propaganda and hate speech as the forces of economic and social precarity intensify. Post-truth politics now appears to be firmly established in American culture; a generation or more would be required to diminish its pernicious influence. Sowing as it does deep mistrust, political untruths (a term we prefer over "misinformation" and "alternative facts") paralyze a participatory politics that would otherwise be geared toward a progressive, innovative governing agenda aimed at enfranchising more people, expanding a great number of political rights, and enhancing economic opportunities in a rapidly transforming national (never mind global) economy.

We define a progressive agenda as one that is capable of meeting pressing governing needs and addressing long-term existential problems like failing schools, the politics of big-money influence, threats to human security, and certainly the climate crisis. In a time of willful ignorance and deliberate confusion for much of the mainstream culture, we should expect the present situation to get worse. In fact, with such massive structures of power already in place, citizens should *prepare* for it to get much worse.

The most immediate task, then, is to formulate a governing alternative. If the forces we have characterized are social and cultural just as much as they are economic and political, counter strategies must offer a vision of a political world that is more just, more humane, and one oriented to a future that can actually be achieved—one that is inclusive and is grounded in a sense of community and social solidarity that crosses racial, ethnic and class lines. The political time is propitious for an advancement on such a front. And if the American right fails to formulate a comprehensive political vision of its own—as it appears determined *not* to do—then a space is available to citizens of another political persuasion to move alternatives forward, alternatives that may, over time, galvanize the citizenry at all levels of society. Doing so will require articulating narratives of political and social life that can bind many different interests and collectivities together.

As we begin to hear more in the years ahead about social democratic alternatives in the American context, we should pay especially close attention to the manner in which the concepts being described are framed in the prevailing political discourse.

How concepts like social democracy travel along with terms like freedom, liberty, individual rights, and "opportunity society" will matter profoundly.

Many Americans were probably caught off guard as they heard Bernie Sanders and Alexandria Ocasio-Cortez invoke the term *social democracy*. This is somewhat understandable. The United States is home to scarcely any tradition of socialism in its politics. This is not to say there have not been murmurings and even forthright invocations of the ideology in the United States over more than a century. In fact, a whole range of measures, including social security, Medicare and Medicaid, banking regulations, collective bargaining and most recently the Affordable Care Act, were all implemented, but they were done so to *preserve* capitalism and stave off calls for more radical reforms. But in terms of party platform, economic organization and the direction of public policy the United States is quite unlike any other major industrialized country. There is no bona fide left-wing flank agitating for extensive planning relative to economic capacities or building more elaborate social safety nets for those disadvantaged by age, ethnicity, race and sexual orientation. This fact alone makes the American experience a most unusual case, even if the present moment represents the start of a gradual transformation toward a viable social democratic alternative.

As such a fraught concept in American political culture, socialism remains easy to dispatch from almost any political discussion. It rarely receives serious consideration in public debate, let alone the mainstream media, because it is thought to be anathema to just about anything quintessentially American. Now, what counts as "American" in the context of most discussions of politics in this country is an exceedingly narrow cultural figment that bears little resemblance to the country's actual experiences with social solidarity and activist government (The New Deal, the Second World War, and the major Great Society programs of the 1960s). Moreover, it should also be acknowledged that socialism has always been a loaded concept in political discourse, a term that goes without saying because it *comes* without saying. One already knows in advance the dark political condemnations the term is destined to absorb. At almost any mention, an entire arsenal of cultural supports is wheeled out to assault the *blaspheme*, eliciting predictable reactions from the predictable corners. Impressions form and elide easily across almost every other political persuasion. Indeed, such responses are so common that one must immediately pivot to the position of reverting to political culture as opposed to, say, those of social justice or political economy when pressed to explain "why there is no socialist tradition in America." The most common arguments suggest that the United States is an "exceptional" nation with outsized power and responsibility, one in full possession of a divinely inspired ideology. Consequently, America's singularly unique cultural and religious attributes mean the country is essentially immune from such a cancerous arrangement.

Socialism is also, of course, a close kin of communism, what is today a far less familiar ideology than it was just a generation ago. Still, along with socialism, communism too remains unusually charged in American political discourse. We must also acknowledge that socialism was ominously joined to the moniker "nationalism" during Germany's Third Reich. Hitler's Nazi Party was defined in terms of a single-party state—with an exceedingly large state apparatus—and a centrally planned economy organized around preparations for war. For our parents' and our grandparents' generations, communism and socialism could only evoke feelings of considerable bitterness and anger. At whatever remove, many from these generations came out of the totalitarian experiments of Soviet Russia. Their experiences also darkly colored their interpretations of the great schism in world politics that ruled during the Cold War. Still, these memories are considerably less prominent today.

Another factor behind Americans' unfamiliarity with socialism—and once more, an element related to political culture—is the way in which the ends of public interest in the United States, namely citizenship, are occluded by private power. Private welfare and the pursuit of wealth—or at least the ideology that proclaims it as being available to all—have swamped issues of equity, the sanctity of personhood, and the political integrity of a national political community. This effectively displaces citizenship as worthy of standing and replaces it with the virtue of individual self-interest, narrowly construed in material terms. This factor is also linked to the cult of exceptionalism, which gives wide sway to market forces and individual commercial success while subordinating one's individuality to matters of a private realm beyond the proper scope of government.

To be sure, there is some truth to the idea that Americans consider themselves less as citizens of a democracy than as a people defined politically through their personal and religious beliefs, especially those associated with the promises of a free-market economy. Beliefs that bear on the collective are basically religious in nature, and that cannot but present a very consequential political casualty. Ideas such as freedom and the free market are usually associated with *capitalism* as some divinely inspired organization of the collective, not with *democracy* as such. Additionally, the liberal tradition in America prioritizes individual rights over social and political obligations. Some conservatives—in the communitarian tradition, for example—have sought to rectify this, but rarely in a way that links citizenship to political economy via a fairer tax system or to the strengthening of social safety nets.

Another factor related to identity is Americans' discomfort with the idea of class. Any hint of a suggestion that class consciousness is at work in the country arouses strident retorts of partisan (or worse, *class*) warfare. But a society that talks incessantly about how it must disavow class consciousness surely suggests that something akin to the reverse is actually at work. Perhaps there is almost a desperate defensiveness in the effort to fend off class as a relevant category, as if the country cannot allow such a dimension to affect policy discussions about access to affordable housing, quality education, low-crime areas, basic health care, environmental security and basic foodstuffs. Just to list these dimensions of the public good (and thus of public policy) is to see how potent the dimension of class really is. It is impossible to imagine any of these realms properly evaluated, let alone addressed in full, without an appreciation of the way in which class shapes access to them in adequate measure.

Then there is the complex matter of political economy. A nation's economy being so determinative of its politics may explain why socialism—to the extent that one *has* a basic understanding of its ideological roots—would be found so contrary to America's political culture. Command economies imply a lack of *business* freedom, and that is thought to translate into a lack of *individual* freedom.

And finally, there is something to the idea that Americans today feel a sense of nervousness about the idea of democracy tout court. If the people theoretically hold the power in a democracy, to what degree are they actually able to exercise it? We accept a great many undemocratic practices that are part and parcel of the nation's institutions. When we dislike them, we are quick with the charge of "elitism" and accusations of the wide sway of "unelected bureaucrats."

Could it be that democratic socialism is viable only in a society that is already persuaded by the validity of uniquely democratic provisions—that broad political enfranchisement is vitally important, and that institutional protections must extend beyond the legal and public policymaking bodies of government; and that they should extend into the culture in order for democracy to remain viable and for the nation's politics to remain healthy enough to last?

In its classical form, socialism advocated a revolutionary politics aimed at upending capitalism. In contrast, social democracy does not oppose an economic system that encourages markets. But Americans are perhaps most in need of envisioning political affairs by way of conceptions that can arouse a participatory politics and inspire citizens to engage more thoughtfully in many aspects of civic life. Social democracy is actually grounded in a pragmatic politics that corresponds to the public's needs in terms of both its politics as well as its economy. When social democracy does this, societal and cultural advantages can be realized. The resources that we argue are available can be used to chart a course through an incredibly fraught set of national circumstances that are very much of our own making. At a time when the promise of a shared national life is so radically called into question, citizens must agitate for reforms that not only serve the least advantaged but can also build trust across groups and restore people's faith that the country can rise to the challenge of huge problems.

In terms of the economy, we endorse Karl Polanyi's mid-twentieth-century claim that social democracy means subordinating the economy to democratic politics. To be clear, this subordination is not made to the *state*, not to the *nation*, and not to *government* per se, but to *democracy*. What this implies is a people developing mechanisms through which the economy can best respond to the needs of all citizens and residents of the polity, enhancing their chances of realizing strong, safe, secure lives, and building resilient communities amidst pressures that emerge from within as well as outside the national geography. It means working hard to ensure that political contestation is healthy, and that political debate stays informed rather than becoming subject to whatever whims and fancies of entrepreneurial opportunists. It implies a participatory politics in which informed people understand they have an obligation to continue their political education throughout their lives, to reflect on the issues and problems the country confronts, and that they are willing to craft compromises, forging unities to build toward a more just, more sustainable, more humane future.

Back in the early twentieth century, European societies faced challenges similar to those America now faces. The difference is that, in these societies, democratic institutions were quite new and untested. The First World War caused such devastation and societal fractures became so deep that democracy was essentially hijacked; nationalists stepped into the emerging social and political void. Again, it pays to revisit that distant era today, for it provides lessons about the challenges democracies will perpetually face, regardless of their age. Americans should not be so reassured that because their democracy seems so old, free and fair elections, checks on power in co-equal branches, a vigilant judiciary and a functioning legal system will stand up and perform while under considerable strain. Compounding the problems associated with the basic task of governing is that the cultural currents—which themselves can and should serve as critical supports for democratic practices—are not disposed to honor the built-in protections afforded by civil rights and liberties. The Supreme Court has already signaled to those in the American South that they are free to trammel upon the ability of citizens to cast ballots without worrying about federal monitoring or oversight. Yet, while the governing ordeal America now faces is very grave, there are many national frameworks and experiments of social democratic engagement to which we can appeal.

If a new political framework is to be constructed, it must address many of the governing challenges the chapters in this book take on. It should *affirm* a moral–ethical and political platform that can seize the space vacated by the right on matters of race relations, gender equity, the economy, environmental stewardship, equal access to the ballot, a more level playing field in terms of campaign financing and independent journalism. But Americans are not well disposed to face the new political landscape they have entered, one that must begin to take shape in moral–ethical terms before any progressive political path can be cut into the future. The obstacles in our way are enormous—among them great confusion about identity, ideology and history, and deep misunderstandings relative to political economy given the juggernaut of American capitalism. There is also an abject failure to account for social and environmental dimensions that should figure much more prominently in political discourse about the fate of public life in a democracy.

The practices of social democracy should work more deliberately to conjoin citizen activism, government power, public policy and a spirit of solidarity among fellow citizens. These practices should aim to bridge the multiple divides that today figure so prominently in American political discourse. When such conjoining occurs above the water line—as with the voter mobilization drives in Georgia, the Black Lives Matter protests, and Occupy Wall Street—a politics grounded in identity claims will meet up against a more formidable foe as ordinary people agitate for a greater share of economic and political power. Identity politics will ebb and recede, to be sure, but if group identities can be folded into political projects that prioritize overarching problems faced by an ever-greater number of people (regardless of minor differences), if it can focus on the failures of past policies and if it can elevate discussions and rise above invidious discourses and actions of identity claimants, perhaps then the grip of far-right politics might be loosened, and a refashioning of Americans' collective political consciousness can get started.

Creating the means by which people will recognize how woefully inadequate government programs are today, and establishing venues through which people can collectively discuss how it is that a vast number of basic needs (access to quality education and decent health and elder care, clean water and air, nondiscrimination in the workplace, etc.) persistently go unmet will, with effort and over time, chip away at the anxiousness so many people feel in adopting narrow group identities and settling for the political qualities associated with narrow conceptions of "true" community. The steady assertion of citizens' basic rights and the agitation of a politics aimed at building toward collective power could then begin to compete with the schizophrenia of Fox and Friends, QAnon and the bile that flows out of countless social media platforms. Who would have thought that "Critical Race Theory" would wind up in the gunsights of the far Right as voter suppression drives reached the courts and state legislatures? This development is yet another illustration of a recurring pattern of incitement by which the far Right advances. Of course, as the acronym CRT has entered political discourse, few have stopped to ask if any of the usual commentators have actually taken the time to *read* any of the scholarship associated with this "school," or to sample at the same time from the wider scholarship of public law. Apparently, it is not enough to have stopped teaching basic civics in the public schools, let alone reading the Constitution. Now students must be protected from the indelicacies of a country whose history includes the enslavement of a considerable part of its labor force, followed by denying them the vote.

We are reminded once again that the Right moves skillfully from hot-button issue to hot-button issue, never staying in one place for very long. But this strategy also represents an important opportunity for the Left. Opposition to measures blocking CRT from school curricula in Texas and Georgia could create another groundswell of citizen activism capable of bringing about an enduring vigilance of its own. Such a lift would be substantial, and the weight would not lessen anytime soon, but it would mean mobilizing people around practical concerns that correspond to legacies of discrimination and racism, and in so doing could work to ground social democratic practices in the efforts of citizens to stand behind and advocate for policies bearing on the national collective, wielding power that is held in common for a reason. The Left might use this strategy more effectively than the Right does, working in advance to anticipate the far Right's insidious next moves and build counter-narratives capable of deflecting attention away *from* the latest Tucker Carlson incitement, say, and *toward* a more meaningful dialogue about investments in public education, infrastructure, equity and inclusion in schools and in the workplace. The "social" of social democracy would thereby receive explicit consideration, and it could potentially elicit responses from more constituencies with actual stakes in public debates and civic actions.

The concept of value pluralism often comes to mind in the context of such discussions—those bearing on competing interests in a democracy. However, we should press much further beyond such a superficial politics loaded with naïve assumptions about the ways in which power courses through society. Practices of collective action as instances of social democracy need not be limited to interest-group striving, supposedly (though most often not) producing a kind of balance of interests vying for space in an unceasing competition for a share of political power. Such efforts unduly constrain the field of political action because they usually end up advocating for a narrow set of special interests—for example, the gun lobby, women's rights, environmental concerns, and so forth. On the Left this has been a persistent problem: LGBTQ politics, racial justice movements, women and other minority rights and environmental advocacy—each deserving of advancement, and all progressive causes—can actually work to limit conversations and actions among these groups. The task is to coalesce them in ways that build strong coalitions that can advance a common governing agenda, one that affirms the citizenry and its necessary relation to legitimate authority in a polity where differences are many and intractable.

It is in fact quite striking how infrequently the concept of citizenship itself comes up in the discussions of democracy that are under assault. This is especially surprising because the political aspects of participatory rule are just as important as economic dimensions of fair economic organization. Perhaps more so. The point is that power must be shared if democratic energies are to be utilized to secure public goods within and across constituencies. There may still be no better example of this than the Affordable Care Act, which has allowed some thirty million Americans access to health insurance for the first time. Many more than this number are now eligible, and many of those who have gained coverage no longer face risks associated with terminal employment, job changes, paying for elders' care, and the like. The Child Tax Credit of the American Rescue Plan (2021)—which increased payments from $2,000 up to $3,000-$3,600 per child per year—is another vital policy measure that appears to be lifting on the order of half of America's children out of poverty.

The larger point is that policy-making advances that improve the quality of life for ordinary Americans should inevitably redound to the political sphere if citizens become more active in combatting exceedingly narrow socio-cultural visions and build awareness of new *experiences* of an improved common life. Such activism in public settings can help to create new expressions of political possibility through solidarity, ones that have the potential to rise above the din of far-Right discourses that so skillfully seize social space, dominate discussions about what is important about that space, and bully would-be interlocuters in social media spheres.

A second (and neglected) area in which citizens can make new inroads lies in reclaiming the Left's commitment to workers, and of the role ordinary working people play in the organization and maintenance of society. Social democracy is rooted historically in advocating for working classes, usually through the advocacy of union organizing and collective bargaining.

We would do well to remember that the Tea Party gained traction during the Obama presidency not by virtue of the appeal to reining in public spending, but because it forged a coalition out of a narrow tranche of the population—mainly 50- and 60-year-old suburban and rural whites—on the basis of an issue that was presented as something held in common and which was allegedly important intergenerationally. As analysts suspected at the time, and as they have demonstrated since, the Tea Party's *raison d'etre* was a racial politics that was masked as public-interest advocacy. Many activists were comfortable, if not quite affluent, citizens who succeeded in radicalizing local and, later on, national politics through public displays of protest. The presence of Tea Party activists at many public events across the country quickly got noticed by media organizations and came to be taken seriously, largely because the group was presented as the work of "grass roots" politics. This form of citizenship appealed to many who could not see below the water line and did not take notice of the rhetoric, which revealed opposition not to government spending, but to a government that *looked* unlike anything activists had much direct experience with. There was also considerable opposition to a government that was inclined to spend revenues, not on foreign wars, but on "takers" and "welfare bums" who did not have "real jobs" or attend the right places of religious worship.

The Occupy Movement of 2010–2012, on the other hand, was a far more transparent grass roots movement. It principally appealed to the young who found America's early 2000s version of capitalism essentially corrupted by the power of big capital. But the Occupy Movement quickly expired because it did not spend nearly enough time and effort to organize for political change at the local, state and national levels. The reason for this was, ostensibly, that many within the movement viewed politics at each level as just about as corrupt as the big banks and auto companies that were bailed out in 2009–2010. Unable to apprehend the power of entrenched interests lobbying for action on the other side, the movement paid dearly for its limited political analysis and what was essentially a utopian vision of change.

There is reason to believe that in the face of a nationwide, indeed global, healthcare crisis, the public measures needed to dampen the spread of the coronavirus might become the basis for more widespread collective mobilization than has been the case with any other national crisis of the past few generations. Unfortunately, the simplest measure of slowing the spread of the virus—vaccination—has itself become subjected to rigidly partisan politics, as if getting inoculated were a vote for Biden and refusing to do so a vote for Trump. At this juncture a potential alliance between healthcare workers, government medical professionals and the citizenry in general will have to be more fully and carefully articulated than it has been so far if we are to avoid letting a lethal virus persist.

Of course, there is no final reckoning on offer, and no easy mediation of the complex forces that now conspire to imperil liberal democracy, thwart the public's civic sense, compromise sentiments of mutual trust and ultimately threaten the health and longevity of the entire polity. Still, there are measures we can take to grasp both what has happened and to identify the mechanisms available to reverse course. Social democracy, we suggest, represents our best hope.

We close with the words of Abraham Lincoln, an American who would not normally be associated with social democracy but whose understanding of politics and citizenship actually embodies that ethos:

> Government is a combination of the people of a country to effect certain objects by joint effort. The best framed and best administered governments are necessarily expensive; while by errors in frame and maladministration most of them are more onerous than they need be, and some of them very oppressive. Why, then, should we have government? Why not each individual take to himself the whole fruit of his labor, without having any of it taxed away, in services, corn, or money?
>
> The legitimate object of government, is to do for a community of people, whatever they need to have done, but can not do, *at all*, or can not, so *well do*, for themselves—in their separate, and individual capacities. There are many things—some of them exist independently of the injustice in the world. Making and maintaining roads, bridges, and the like; providing for the helpless young and afflicted; common schools; and disposing of deceased men's property, are instances.
>
> In all that the people can individually do as well for themselves, government ought not to interfere.
>
> *("Fragments on Government," The Writings of Abraham Lincoln, p. 57)*

Bibliography

Baldwin, J. (1965) "James Baldwin vs. William F Buckley: A legendary debate from 1965," www.youtube.com/watch?v=5Tek9h3a5wQ

Brown, W. (2017) *Undoing the Demos: Neoliberalism's Stealth Revolution*, New York: Zone Books.

Connolly, W.E. (1991) *Identity\Difference: Democratic Negotiations of Political Paradox*, Ithaca: Cornell University Press.

Connolly, W.E. (2019) *Climate Machines, Fascist Drives and Truth*, Durham: Duke University Press.

Financial Times, 3 April 2020: www.ft.com/content/7eff769a-74dd-11ea-95fe-fcd274e920ca.

Frieden, J.A. (2020) *Global Capitalism: Its Fall and Rise in the Twentieth Century, and Its Stumbles in the Twenty-first,* New York: W.W. Norton.

Hochschild, A.R. (2018) *Strangers in Their Own Land: Anger and Mourning on the American Right*, New York: The New Press.
Judis, J. (2020) *The Socialist Awakening: What's Different Now about the Left*, New York: Columbia Global Reports.
Judt, T. (2011) *Ill Fares the Land*, New York: Penguin.
Lincoln, A. (2012) *The Writings of Abraham Lincoln*, edited by Steven B. Smith, New Haven: Yale University Press.
Polanyi, K. (2001) *The Great Transformation: The Political and Economic Origins of Our Time*, Boston: Beacon Press.
Wolin, S.S. (1987) *The Presence of the Past: Essays on the State and the Constitution*, Princeton: Princeton University Press.

6
PANDENOMICS

The coronavirus pandemic has never been just a global public-health disaster. It brought with it enormous social and political dislocation that will have broad societal ramifications, not only for those individuals and families afflicted directly with the virus, but also for the wider communities around them. The impact will radiate out extensively to include all areas of society: from those who have tendered public-health support and labored in elder-care facilities, to the countless laborers whose essential work of food preparation and package delivery has made it possible for vast sectors of the population to remain relatively removed and isolated from the most immediate biological impact of the virus. Beyond the immediate threat of direct exposure, the pandemic has made itself known through the increased risk of homelessness for those who have lost incomes, the unavailability of everyday medical care and emergency treatment for non-COVID cases as ICUs filled up and nurses became overwhelmed, and the long-term impact that school closures and compromised educational opportunities have had on an entire generation of young people.

In looking at the broad impacts, we discern some areas that have an influence on the ability of citizens to act and engage constructively in their political communities. In important respects, some of the foundations of democratic participation are likely to be eroded by changing habits and life patterns brought about in the aftermath of the pandemic. At the same time, we think that the pandemic itself has exposed practices that help us understand the scope of social and political redress needed if societies are to learn from their failings and restore confidence in the public purpose in a post-pandemic world.

When a virus strikes worldwide, infecting as it did 175 million people by mid-2021 and claiming 3.8 million lives within the first sixteen months, we must rise to the challenges posed by a host of dramatic social consequences. Certainly the

DOI: 10.4324/9781003268741-7

United States must confront a great number of shortcomings in leadership and ideology when—again, by mid-2021—over 34 million Americans tested positive for COVID-19, resulting in over 615,000 deaths. The U.S. death rate of 1,848 per million was 3.8 times the world average. It was exceeded (marginally) by Argentina (1,856), Great Britain (1,875), Poland (1,971) and Croatia (1992). Other countries exceeded it by more than marginally: Italy (2,103), Belgium (2,155), Brazil (2,272) and all the rest of the Eastern Europe and Balkan states (2,117–3,103). The one stunning outlier, evidence of a collapsed healthcare system, has been Peru (5,631).

By comparison, the U.S. death rate is 2.7 times greater than Canada's, 7 times India's and 17 times that of Japan's ("Corona Virus Update," *Worldometer*, June 12, 2021).

The impacts of the virus are spread unevenly around the globe. In the countries most heavily hit by the pandemic the disruptions wrought by the virus are extensive, to be understood not only in terms of fatalities and hospitalizations but also in the measures required to adjust everyday life so that the toll would not be even larger. The biggest difference in the tenor of life in those countries that were spared the worst ravages of the virus is that the social measures needed to tamp down the virus were taken early on, with decisive government intervention and popular compliance such that countries like Australia, New Zealand and South Korea could manage to open back up relatively quickly after periods of shutdown.

The gross data tell us little about the quality of life during a pandemic. They suggest nothing about what the long-term impact of the pandemic might be, especially on those countries like the United States and UK, where the effects have been protracted and subject to recurring waves of severity and to the relative laxity of their national governments. Understandably, governments have scrambled to soften the impact of social dislocation and shutdown through a variety of subsidies and regulatory policies. As with any pre-existing inequality, the effects of such aid have been to compound and, in many cases, intensify that inequity.

The economic consequences of the pandemic are at one level ultimately measurable by easily accessed standard macroeconomic indicators like unemployment rates, lost wages, consumer spending, impact on Gross Domestic Product and government expenditures. Yet these familiar metrics, so common in news coverage, convey precious little absent any sense of what it means for citizens to go through the agony of unemployment, lost wages, rent squeezes, homelessness and having to make decisions about whether one can buy food or must resort to a charity food line. Even for those who managed to maintain a work life, adjusting to completely altered home conditions—overseeing kids attending online classes or being separated from loved ones for long periods of time—changed a great number of societal dynamics well beyond standard work-life management. The burden on women has been especially severe, many of whom had additional domestic responsibilities heaped upon demands already experienced by managing careers. For those with parents in elder care there has been a whole new level of stress in terms of the living conditions and services available at assisted-living and nursing-care facilities. Nor do such effects go away even with a declared end of the pandemic, given how the elderly are subject to an irreversible decline in physical health and cognitive acuity once they are removed from their normal routines and forced into isolation. For senior citizens, social distancing can be a slow-motion death sentence that does not register as a COVID-19 fatality.

For single parents, the adjustment to a year or more of monitoring and management took an enormous toll. For married couples suddenly required to compress their lives into a confined domestic space, the result cannot have been simple or fully anticipated. It brought couples together in ways that for some were welcome and for many others, complex and fraught with tension. It certainly brought the increased likelihood of domestic abuse—a trend confirmed by recent statistics. So, too, suicide rates across the country increased. Crime rates and murder rates were also generally on the rise—functions, no doubt, of increased frustration, despair over increased impoverishment and impatience with the pace at which life might return to normal.

And what might that "normal" look like? We got a fleeting glimpse of it in early 2021. No sooner was there a back-to-work movement in the wake of the vaccine rollouts than it became clear that the post-pandemic era would not look like the pre-pandemic one. Ongoing discussions about economic recovery do little to illuminate the character of what lies ahead. The models of supply and demand, income and spending, tax rates and tax revenues, are all generally based on formal economic models of a business cycle. None of that tells us what the post-pandemic world will bring in terms of attitudes about the responsibilities of citizens to one another and their government. Nor is it likely that we will ever crawl out from under the threat of some sort of recurring viral pandemic; there are too many variants of the COVID-19 around and too many opportunities for another virus-like scare to reappear.

It goes without saying that the public issues and social fractures that characterized the world pre-pandemic will shape the outcomes in a post-pandemic era. That was immediately made evident in the rollout of the Pfizer and Moderna vaccines, when issues of access and distribution arose and intensified existing power rifts to reveal, if not to deepen, certain cultural biases toward science and government.

The advent of vaccines with plus/minus 95-percent efficacy was initially heralded in late 2020 as a sign of substantive scientific achievement—a breakthrough in the normally slower, more painstaking pace of biomedical research and development, which usually sees results accrue over decades. The accelerated pace of development was one of the few things the Trump Administration could claim credit for as a positive development, though the precise mechanism by which "Operation Warp Speed" expedited private sector research and development in this case was never at all clear. Ironically, the one area of unrefuted government expeditiousness in the process of getting the vaccines through from trials into production and distribution was a highly compressed approvals process by the Food and Drug Administration. The White House had been putting intense pressure on all involved to get a vaccine out by Election Day 2020 because aides felt it would increase the president's re-election chances. When the vaccines did not materialize in time, Trump still pressured officials to push for quick approval on an emergency basis. Doing so made it seem as if the technical process of meticulously analyzing the vaccine trials for safety was being politicized—which was the last thing public health officials wanted. The fast-tracking of the whole process has probably contributed to a sense among some vaccine skeptics and government critics that the COVID-19 vaccines were somehow less reliable than drugs normally developed for the market. That, in turn, surely contributed to the reluctance of some in the populace to take the vaccine at all. That sensitivity about the approvals process appeared to gain ballast a few months later when the third greenlighted vaccine, Johnson & Johnson's AstraZeneca version, was put on temporary hold while medical officials investigated reports of an extremely rare blood clot condition associated with the drug. It turned out statistically to be much ado about virtually nothing—a naturally occurring condition that appears with miniscule frequency and turns out not to be induced by the vaccine.

Initially the vaccine rollout was slower than first promised, thanks to the sheer scale of it, the challenge of having to store the Pfizer vaccine at minus 70 degrees Celsius, and the administrative structure required to assign and oversee eligibility for the inoculations. There was no centralized, federal plan in place by the outgoing administration for distribution, education and injections. Instead, it was left up to the states, each with its own infrastructure, though generally following CDC guidelines for signing up, with frontline healthcare workers qualifying first along with long-term care facility residents and medical first responders. Next in line would be those 75 years of age and older along with residents and staffs of group living facilities: shelters, prisons and treatment centers.

It quickly became apparent that these delineations were quite porous, and that the flow and processing of people varied dramatically from state to state. Moreover, the mechanics of securing an appointment for those not in sheltered homes required considerable Internet dexterity and patience—which is not a class-neutral skill and calls for, among other things, web familiarity, a good Internet connection and the considerable free time needed to deploy it.

The vaccination campaign was hampered at the start by other things as well: a combination of political, epidemiological and cultural factors requiring careful planning by governments and private administrators to manage properly.

By the time the vaccines were in circulation in the early weeks of 2021 at least three partial mutations of the COVID-19 virus appeared, each with slightly different characteristics and proclivities for spreading. The English, South African and Brazilian variants could still be handled by the vaccines, studies suggested, though efficacy appeared to be marginally lower. With the initial rollout slow and the mutations working their way across the globe, as they inevitably do by crossing borders and oceans, it was only a matter of time before those infected with these more aggressive variants would lead to a spike in the infection rate—across the

Northern hemisphere in mid-winter, no less—and undo the progress being made in stabilizing test-positivity rates and hospitalizations. The only way to outrun the tendency of viruses to develop variants is to reduce the availability of bodies with the potential to become infected. It was a simple math problem of demographics: shrinking the supply of targetable people by developing antibodies in as many as possible so that the pool of potential victims shrinks at a greater rate than the growth-rate of infections. The path to herd immunity, it turns out, is an unsteady one, even under the best of conditions.

It did not help that a certain percentage of eligible people simply turned down the vaccine altogether. Mistrust along racial lines is no less rampant in public health than in any other sector of society. There is, for example, a well-publicized history of the (white) medical community mistreating peoples of color through covert experimentation without permission, such as the forty-year-long Tuskegee Study of untreated syphilis in Black men. There are also more subtle forms of bias tied to the medical community's structural failure to take non-white people seriously when they report symptoms or show signs of illness. In some cases, it is the measuring equipment, like those that record oxygenation level on the basis of surface contact but that do not accurately read data gleaned from dark-toned skin. In other cases, it is a more complex phenomenon of "healthcare deserts" and a shortage of pharmacies in major urban centers where people of color predominate. One outcome is clear, however; widespread suspicion by peoples of color towards the intentions and practices of the medical community makes it difficult to state the case for those healthcare measures that would benefit all, equally. Compounding the problem is the historic reluctance to engage formal medical help due to the long-term consequences of poverty; when you have managed for decades to avoid seeing doctors except on the basis of an emergency room visit, you learn to make due, for better or worse, without preventive care or regular checkups and monitoring. The data for early rollout confirmed evidence of a race bias, however unintentional, with white populations getting vaccinated at disproportionately higher rates of the population than those from communities of color. The healthcare community has been playing catchup since the outset of the vaccine program.

Education, access and basic communication can help overcome some of these barriers, but that requires determined efforts, especially because the issue of racial inequity in medical service overlaps with that of class bias as well. The poor cannot afford medical service and learn to do without it. They also learn not to trust those who represent the medical community. This dynamic was evident, for example, in the initial reluctance of healthcare workers at nursing homes and assisted living facilities to get inoculated when they became eligible. Initial uptake rates were at the 30–40 percent levels—and this among frontline employees most exposed on a regular basis to the demographic that is most susceptible to COVID-19 infection, the elderly. If this seems irrational, consider that the healthcare workers at these elder-care facilities generally work for minimum wage, with limited if any healthcare benefits at all. To make matters worse, these workers were also expected to report for work during the early stages of the pandemic in 2020 without being provided PPE or access to regular testing. If they were sick, they were not eligible for sick leave, so even those employees who were infected with the virus often found themselves forced, out of economic necessity, to show up for work. And now they are suddenly expected to accept at face value the assurance that the vaccine they were being offered would benefit them.

While the pandemic and the subsequent vaccine campaign revealed existing social rifts and antagonisms, they also deepened those class antagonisms in ways that further complicated efforts to resolve the crisis. The pandemic has been an accelerator of economic inequality. Rich people got richer and poor people have been getting poorer, with the middle class shrinking and for the most part sinking. Minimum wage levels had not been keeping up with the cost of living for years while the bulk of federally mandated tax breaks over the last forty-plus years has gone to those with large assets. This has left millions more of the working poor falling behind, sometimes juggling two and three part-time jobs or clinging to retail and frontline food service work as they struggled to keep families afloat.

When the pandemic hit in the late winter of 2020 and led to the initial wave of shutdowns by early spring, many of those in economically marginal positions were the first to go. The initial impact on the workplace was severe: thirty million Americans were suddenly out of work. The low end of the hospitality trades—room cleaners, kitchen staff, wait staff and busboys—was especially hard hit. Large-scale entertainment arenas and theaters also shuttered, leaving their food, cleaning and service staffs to be laid off. For these laborers there was no option of working from home. Likewise, for those in the transportation sector, as public busses and trains emptied out and other people stayed home rather than flitting about in cabs or via Uber. Teachers could shift to instruction from home; denizens of the vast digital design, legal, editorial and marketing sectors could adjust through Zoom, Webinars and Workspace. These options were not available to front-line service workers, many of whom were furloughed. To a considerable extent, new opportunities opened up in direct delivery service, whether for drivers of Amazon or those doing the food shopping and delivery for the likes of Instacart or DoorDash. The latter jobs required access to a reliable car—not a simple matter for the working poor. Meanwhile, long-haul truck drivers quickly made the transition to short-haul, local delivery service because it allowed them to keep working while spending nights at home. The result was a nationwide shortage of long-haul truckers, leading to delays in delivery and crippling interruptions in supply chains.

Those furloughed from private companies and non-profits were able to benefit from temporarily enhanced unemployment benefits—though even here, eligibility varied from county to county and state to state. When those enhanced benefits ran out for many by the end of the summer of 2020 (not to be restored until 2021) many people were still left to fend for themselves. A temporary halt to student loan repayment helped, as did rules prohibiting eviction—though the latter were very unevenly enforced.

The point is that, suddenly, a vast swath of ordinary working Americans experienced complete dislocation. In most municipalities, people who normally could send their kids off to school were now also saddled with overseeing their attendance in online classes—no easy feat for the parents of pre-teens or, for that matter, adolescents.

Government relief in the form of a $1,200 check to individuals earning under $75,000 annually or couples earning $150,000 certainly helped ameliorate the worst of the disruption. But this one-time benefit was well below subsidies available in the majority of other advanced industrial democracies. And it did not come close to making up for the lost wages and tips that impacted low-wage workers. Moreover, as popular as the direct family payment was, it obscured most of the deeper politics of the $2 trillion Coronavirus Aid, Relief and Economic Security (CARES) Act passed in May 2020. Only 30 percent of the stimulus package went to individuals in the form of direct payment or unemployment subsidies. A quarter of the package ($500 billion) went to large corporations in the form of low-interest loans or bailouts (for airlines, for example) often without dictates stipulating that the monies had to be used to reach employees. Many large firms used these funds to buy back stock shares or invest in new infrastructure without guarantees of direct benefit to employees. A fifth of the package, totaling $377 billion, was meant to target small businesses, though the application process became rife with corruption and unaccountability, with many otherwise eligible small entities left without access. The remaining 25 percent of the relief package, a share that came to just over $500 billion, went for state and local municipalities and for hospitals, food banks and veterans. Even with this aid, however, state and local governments saw a net loss of revenue, with deficits mounting due to lost income tax revenue and additional expenditures for schools, unemployment, police and healthcare.

The biggest burden of the pandemic economy fell disproportionately on the poor, those in the service sector, and upon municipalities in general. Meanwhile, select elements of the private sector had loan opportunities available, while those in the direct marketing side reaped a windfall from increased traffic. When Republicans refused to support a major follow up aid bill at the end of 2020, supplemental and CARES Act provisions ended; 12 million Americans lost their unemployment benefits and had to reapply under state guidelines subject to bureaucratic overload as application networks crashed due to the demand. Moreover, the lapse of federal guarantees led to millions of people anxious about the threat of eviction due to accumulated unpaid back rent. Student loan moratoria also faced elimination, threatening those with educational debt to have to resume payments. Even as subsequent relief arrived at the last minute to restore a minimum of (temporary) ease, the recurring anxiety and uncertainty took its toll on the most dependent classes of citizens, undermining hopes for the kind of equanimity that is supposed to underpin middle-class life.

Each of these obstacles in the path of the poor proves yet another point, namely that poverty is very expensive emotionally, physically and financially. It is not surprising that when government fails, folks feel frustrated, alienated, outraged and apathetic. They become inclined to check out or become radicalized and lash out against "the system," the "deep state," ultimately imperiling the government's ability to respond in a time of great need.

The popularity of the pandemic relief bills as measured in public opinion surveys has largely been based upon the direct benefits that accrue to everyday Americans. That is also why widespread support for enhanced benefits in 2021—on the order of $1,400 per eligible recipient, in addition to $600 already in the works for that coming year—became a campaign issue in the special Georgia Senate runoff elections in January 2021. Endorsing the initiative was a factor in the ability of the two Democratic insurgents to defeat the two Republican incumbents, both of whom opposed the expanded second stimulus package. In a curious way, however, the popularity of the direct family payment obscured how the deeper politics of the first stimulus package had little to do with alleviating income imbalances.

The Biden Administration's efforts, with the support of the Democratic delegations in the House and Senate, appeared more willing to attach redistributive elements to the $2 billion stimulus package initiated early in the new, 2021 legislative session. The package expanded direct payments to families and included considerably more direct aid to municipalities to offset their budget deficits. It also included extensive aid to states and municipalities for COVID-19 vaccination programs. The result would be to lessen the tax burden that states might otherwise have imposed on their residents. And yet on one crucial point of equity, the Biden-proposed plan had to give way to a remnant of conservative ideological purity. A hike (via stages) in the federal hourly minimum wage from $7.25 to $15 proved too much of an ask. The rate for now would remain pegged to where it was in 2009—all while billionaires continued to reap accumulated riches from the combination of recent tax reform, pandemic recovery subsidies and new business.

Not surprisingly, Republicans in the House and Senate objected to the bulk of the stimulus package on the basis of—once again—cooked up concern about growing federal deficits. This arose after they had easily handed out more than $700 billion in tax relief to upper income earners during the Trump Administration. The sudden re-discovery of old-fashioned conservative budgetary prudence struck most observers (and much of the public) as brazen hypocrisy. Class warfare has never been absent in Washington politics and played no small role here in drawing the lines about the size of a stimulus package. What often gets lost in the public drama—especially as militant anti-democracy and white supremacy activists assert themselves—is the extent to which class issues get sublimated and reconfigured into a split between democratic populism on the one hand and authoritarian populism on the other.

The pandemic's consequences continue to play out internationally with dramatic effect, with some of the hardest-hit developing countries being particularly ravaged due to limited medical infrastructure. Unfortunately, the advent of vaccines will not have much effect in these countries for some time. Indeed, we are likely to see a widening rift between the have and have-not countries when it comes to access to the vaccine. Great Britain, Canada, the United States and the European Union grabbed the vast majority of the vaccine's early release; 49 countries controlled 39 million doses while Guinea held exactly 25 doses in total. Inequities like that led World Health Organization director general Tedros Adhanom Ghebreyesus to denounce what he characterized as "vaccine nationalism."

This gap in availability is tied to the ability to pay, as well as to the distribution of research development and manufacturing power in the global system. It exacerbates the already considerable worldwide gap in wealth, health, quality of life and ability of states to manage their environmental affairs. Someone has to pay for the vaccine; someone has to gain access to supplies and distribution networks. Poor, developing countries and those with non-functioning states or outright authoritarian regimes will not be able or willing to develop the capacity to inoculate their populations in sufficient numbers to produce widespread immunity. When developing countries like India face sudden surges in demand for hospital facilities, oxygen and healthcare because of outbreaks in COVID-19 (like the one that ravaged the country in the spring of 2021), they end up relying on charitable handouts rather than functioning markets for goods and services in the world economy. These countries lack budgets, purchasing power and infrastructure for the necessary preventive measures. This condition will make life in those countries more precarious than ever. Increasingly, we will see problems spill over into so-called advanced economies given the likely flow of refugees from state violence, civil unrest and resource conflicts.

Back home, our everyday lives would be very different no matter how soon the vaccines became widely adopted. As of late 2021 there has already been a dramatic shift to online shopping—witness the daily parade of UPS, USPS and Amazon delivery trucks in almost any neighborhood. Brick-and-mortar shopping, already under stress over the last few years, will accelerate in its decline. This trend will not go away, and while in-store browsing and shopping will enjoy something of a return as the pandemic's grip eases, the secular trend, which was accelerated by recent developments, means that any post-pandemic retail culture will be far more online than it was before. There will always be a place for smaller, boutique retail. But the shift will prove near-fatal for the kind of mid-tier commerce that takes place at shopping malls, with more of these closing each year and likely headed towards converted-use facilities as senior-living centers or healthcare or lifestyle centers for the affluent.

Meanwhile, big-box stores like Walmart, Costco, Whole Foods and Home Depot will continue to flourish because they offer the kind of large-scale shopping at discount prices and/or seamless convenience that have been destroying mid-level shops for decades. We are likely to see a further concentration of the marketing system, which means depressed wages over the long term and a loss of entrepreneurial ownership as a basic skill set of the economy. The consequences for the cultivation of citizenship engagement will be widespread and could be devastating at many levels.

Much of rural America is in serious trouble. Town centers under pressure from a loss of commercial life are giving way to big-box stores that have been built anew, often with generous local tax concessions, and out on an isolated stretch of land nowhere near where people were ever prone to gather—though at least convenient to a highway exit. That has already meant a considerable loss in the ability of people to meet, talk and engage each other in the ways that are so crucial to building a sense of community and a civic ethos. The trends across the American West are unmistakable, not only in Native American communities but across the prairie lands and many farm communities—as it already has been across Appalachia due to the collapse of traditional industries like furniture, textile manufacturing and coal mining. Add to these economic pressures the fateful consequences of overwhelmed, understaffed rural healthcare systems, and one sees the country faces a formula for depopulation. With it goes the decline of basic medical services as HMOs consolidate, solo practitioners find it harder to thrive, and as small-town clinics and hospitals close. All of this has a deflationary effect on housing, savings and retirement. A sense of frustration and personal impotence comes to replace what once might have been a feeling of hopefulness about building a better future for oneself and one's family, such as existed for many after the Second World War.

With media outlets nationalizing under the influence of cable TV and the concentration of ever larger newspaper and magazine conglomerates, local news has been devastated. The once-profitable, standard sources of revenue for these outlets—classifieds and display advertising for newsprint, and local marketers for TV news—have either gone over to the Web via eBay, Etsy and Facebook or they have been subject to nationalized ad accounts. The drying up of these local revenue streams has led to a loss of local news outlets—and with it, a loss of contact with one's immediate surroundings. This has removed one of the most powerful intermediate networks of social life and civil society by separating people from their locality and nationalizing them in a way that is socially paralyzing. Among the many losses politically is a sense of accountability that local power brokers had to the community. If nobody knows what they are doing, and there is little understanding of the relationship between what they do and who is affected, we all stand to lose out from the standpoint of daily citizenship practices. The pernicious effect this has on the decline of everyday political practice is considerable. The temptation becomes powerful to replace that loss with a level of engagement keyed to the newfound sources of mobilization and messaging available through dark websites and conspiratorial social networks that offer the promise of action and redemption.

One demographic trend worth noting that has accelerated during the pandemic and will continue to do so in its aftermath is the move to enclosed residential enclaves. City enters emptied out as residents with the means to escape found refuge elsewhere, primarily in enclosed outposts, often behind privately guarded gated communities—or simply in open air Bohemian Groves safely isolated from the day-to-day grit of everyday urban concentration. Both trends—towards all-inclusive residential communities and the flight towards super-high-income neighborhoods and zip codes—represent a loss of the cornucopia character of the modern urban experience. The creation of this "barbed wire chic" entails extreme privatization, a retreat from public spaces and from the daily encounters with diversity and complexity by which difference, multiple identities and tolerance are cultivated. It becomes increasingly difficult for privileged citizens to appreciate the complex negotiations needed to maintain diversity, and it detracts from the ability of the country to hold onto, never mind honor, community, engagement and public commitment.

The pandemic did not create this problem. But it has accelerated a long-term secular trend and it has given people an enhanced sense of the precarity of security and safety in time of crisis. Thus, it is likely to remain in force long after the shroud of the pandemic has lifted, and it will shape—or deform—the ability of the country to inculcate truly democratic norms long thereafter. The extreme nesting and self-reliance cultivated in 2020 are not going to disappear. In fact, we appear headed toward more privatization and more isolation from the kinds of engaged civic interactions that had previously characterized our lives.

It also needs to be noted that the ability of the American political system in particular to endure is predicated upon some version of a reasonable balance between the less populated states and the more populous ones. That was the basis for the original division of Congress, with populated states getting proportional representation in the House, and in the Senate the less-populated states getting representation equal to big states. Similar apportionment rules animate the Electoral College, where the ruling principle for determining the size of each state's delegation is House seats plus Senate. As we move ahead, we are going to see greater imbalance than ever in geographical distribution, with cities and suburbs swelling while rural America empties out. Statistically, the imbalance is growing. In the 1870 U.S. census, the first one conducted without the infamous three-fifths clause by which slaves were counted only as 60 percent of a person, the three most populous states outweighed the three least populated states by a factor of forty to one. In 2020, that ratio was forty-seven to one.

This is going to exaggerate the inequities in power whereby a Wyoming or South Dakota has the same voice in the Senate's approval of legislation and nominations as New York or California. The inequity is growing, and the difficulty of adapting to a more representative legislative and electoral system will remain an impediment to good government, producing a built-in reactionary drag effect at the national level. It is going to lead to more distorted outcomes, like a Supreme Court that does not reflect the population's diversity of opinion or identities, with particular distortions in the extent to which the nine justices are more male, whiter, more Catholic and more conservative than the public at large. It will also continue to lead to presidential elections in which candidates winning a majority of votes will still lose in the Electoral College. In fact, Republicans are the beneficiaries of the system, to the extent that while the Democratic presidential candidate outpolled the Republican nominee in seven of the last eight national elections, the Republican candidate still won three of those eight, including two with an electoral minority (in 2000 and 2016).

All of this contributes to a political culture that is increasingly partisan, disengaged across the (metaphoric) aisle, and less emotionally invested in exploring alternatives than it is keen to reinforce its own bias and proclivities. It also sets up the conditions by which extremism can take root and appear to be normal or acceptable and within the bounds of everyday political culture—even as it sets out to destroy that very culture. It will take considerable efforts by the guardians of democracy—citizens—to shore up those practices and to inoculate institutions and practices that affirm rather than erode that commitment.

The most foundational commitment would simply be an aggressive defense and expansion of voting rights, making it easier for the public to exercise its most minimal participatory function, rather than making it more difficult.

Perhaps the most powerful result of the pandemic will simply be to have enhanced an appreciation for our friends and neighbors and the safety of one's community. That extends across the board, from mask wearing and social distancing to a willingness to put up with the increased role of government in managing a healthcare crisis and in investing money into the economy to stave off collapse. If those sentiments and that kind of respect can be cultivated, we will have a chance to offset some of the more insidious developments of the "pandeconomy."

Bibliography

Worldometer (2021). "Corona Virus Update," June 12.

7
BEYOND A MOMENTARY INTERVENTION

It is easy to forget how close we came to losing the country entirely. A momentary indulgence in analytical journalism will help us recall the threat we faced so that we can explore the extent of the effort needed to make sure we do not approach that path again.

It was the week of the November 3, 2020, election. After initial disappointment and much uncertainty on election night, with the majority of American voters issuing nothing close to a decisive repudiation of the Trump presidency, a period of nervous tabulating of mail-in ballots and waiting began. This was followed by an announcement from all the major U.S. media outlets on Saturday, November 7, that former Vice President Joseph R. Biden had secured a majority of the nation's 538 electoral votes and was now the president elect. He would be sworn in as the country's 46th President on January 20, 2021.

Across the country, jubilation set in, with car horns sounding in many cities, dance parties breaking out in the streets, and people showing the kind of exhilaration normally seen in countries that have just overthrown a dictator. Meanwhile, it was clear that Donald Trump would not accept the outcome and was determined to resist conceding defeat, though just how far he might go in refusing to participate in the peaceful transition of power was a matter of open speculation. The possible scenarios ran the gamut, from retreat into a depressive cowering to full-scale martial law to provoking some apocalyptic civil-war crisis.

For those looking for a suitably absurd "opera bouffe" example of a flailing would-be tyrant who is more bluster than substance, the curious case of a displaced press conference that Saturday seemed to offer a paradigmatic example.

Late that morning, after the initial media call of Biden's electoral win, Trump tweeted out news that presaged an adamant defense of his right to protest the outcome of the election. He let his 80 million Twitter followers know about

DOI: 10.4324/9781003268741-8

an important press conference to be held that day, led by his personal legal counsel, former New York City Mayor Rudolph Giuliani. The press conference would unveil the Trump campaign's legal strategy in contesting the election outcome. However, in calling upon the press to attend, Trump inadvertently communicated the wrong site for the announcement. It seems he intended to hold a media conference at the upscale Four Seasons Hotel in downtown Philadelphia. But he accidentally tweeted out the name of the site as "Four Seasons Total Landscaping."

Here is where the ensuing fiasco gets interesting in a way that was not explored in the flurry of news coverage that followed. The landscaping firm Trump referenced in his tweet occupied a desultory industrial site ten miles northeast of downtown Philadelphia. The company works out of a garage and storage area next door to a crematorium on one side and a sex toys shop on the other. Any of Trump's aids could have warned him of the mistake and asked him to tweet corrected instructions. In this White House, however, aids were afraid all along to correct the President for fear of appearing disloyal. And so, true to a fascist epistemology that seeks to will the truth even when it bears no relationship to reality, his staff scrambled mightily to book the landscaping company for the press conference and make it look as though that is what they had intended all along. The lesson here was that even if you know it is not true, act as though it is and make it appear real.

Except that now Giuliani and his legal team were relegated to standing in front of a large garage door festooned with hastily posted Trump signs. The scene was right out of the long-running HBO series "VEEP." Worse for Giuliani, the British comedic satirist Sasha Baron Cohen had just the week before released his follow-up parody of American political culture, *Borat Subsequent Moviefilm*, comprising one outrageous spoof of American political culture after another. In one scene, a very intent if entirely unromantic Giuliani is shown leaning back in the bed of his hotel room with his hand down his pants as he is talking up a young female journalist who had just finished interviewing him.

In moments of political absurdity like these it is one thing to make light of such bumbling incompetence. The "Four Seasons Total Landscaping" escapade was rightly the butt of political mockery the entire weekend. It was also a reminder of the gap between the president's authoritarian aspirations on the one hand and how hideous and hollow his fantasies of power appear in retrospect once they fail. More reassuring is when grandiose plans collapse spectacularly. In this context one might recall some of the old fascist landmarks of Nazi Germany. Chief among them is the *Reichsparteitagsgelände*, a sprawling field where Hitler held Nazi party rallies and where filmmaker Leni Riefenstahl shot the famous propaganda movie, *Triumph of the Will*. Among the features of this vast grounds was a stadium built by Hitler to receive surrendering world leaders. For 40 years that Nuremberg stadium lay reduced to rubble and served as a municipal dumping ground for impounded automobiles. Such are the ruins of despotic fantasy.

That is, when they fail the test of contemplation—a reckoning of what is truly terrifying and not mere absurdist blathering. Which is how many Americans spent the days following the Biden-Harris victory. The press and social media were filled with all sorts of downward spiraling scenarios, most of them culminating in some version of an electoral void into which a resurgent Trump might seize the reins of power to reclaim his office or effect a constitutional crisis whereby Congress (with Supreme Court assent) would maneuver the approval of a dissident slate of state electors pledged to Trump. Or, at the very least—according to other dystopian plot lines—Trump could sabotage American democracy in the weeks before inauguration and leave the country ungovernable, on the veritable edge of a civil war. All of this in the midst of a pandemic.

The signs of a disruptive transition phase from Trump to Biden were palpable, threatening to violate what had been a hallmark of American exceptionalism for over 200 years—the peaceful transfer of power from one administration to the next, regardless of party or politics. Even more remarkable was that Republican lawmakers refused to confront the outgoing president's claims of a stolen election and persisted on a path that helped throw into question the legitimacy of the election and of the Biden presidency. A *Washington Post* survey done in late November/early December 2020 of all 249 sitting Republican senators and representatives found that only 25 of them would acknowledge that Biden had won the election. Most held on to the incumbent president's right to pursue every avenue of legal–political recourse, even if it meant a string of frivolous lawsuits that the courts were summarily throwing out. A large swath of Trump supporters saw a conspiracy in the works to deny their candidate re-election. The campaign even solicited funds from supporters for a legal defense fund, to which one particularly enthusiastic Senate colleague, Lindsay Graham from South Carolina, pledged half a million dollars. Within a month of the election, that fund grew to over $200 million, with donors (many of them contributing in small amounts) having been told that the funds might be used for a variety of political purposes and not just legal electoral defense efforts.

A Trump appointee with the General Services Administration refused for weeks to approve a standard flow of funds to pay transition costs for office space, salaries and utilities. The ritual of the outgoing president greeting the incoming president in the Oval Office—as Obama had done with Trump four years earlier, within days of the election—was abandoned. More ominous as evidence of the personal fealty to Trump was a series of summary firings of key officials in the highest ranks of the military and intelligence services. Mark Esper, Secretary of Defense, had staked out a position during the summer that opposed the president's use of the military in domestic contexts, such as protests. Trump tweeted out Esper's dismissal right after the election. Also on the chopping block were the undersecretary of defense for policy, the undersecretary of defense for intelligence and the chief of staff to the secretary of defense. For good reason this was referred to as a "decapitation" of the U.S. national security apparatus (*Time Magazine*, November 11, 2020).

In each case, these officials were replaced by Trump loyalists on an "acting" basis, which meant they did not need Congressional approval and who, because of their prior avowals of various conspiracy theorists and involvement with shady groups, would probably not have secured approval—or, in the case of the acting defense secretary, had been forced to withdraw his name from earlier consideration. John Tata, the new undersecretary of defense for policy, had earlier denounced Obama as "a terrorist leader" and had openly talked of an assassination plot against John Brennan, the former CIA director. This last-minute shuffling of key appointees was not a mere chess game or a way of rewarding loyalists. The full import would become appallingly evident in early January, when some of these same Defense Department officials botched the calling up of supplemental military support when the Capitol Building came under attack during the Trump-incited riots of January 6, 2021. Only a detailed congressional investigation could determine whether the delayed response was a function of incompetence or of deliberate mishandling. But clearly, the personnel responding to desperate calls for help from Capitol Hill police and from the offices of Vice President Mike Pence and Speaker of the House Nancy Pelosi were not comfortable making operational decisions in the absence of definitive guidance from the White House.

Nor would these be the last firings in the final days of the Trump Administration. Sure enough, when the director of the Department of Homeland Security's Cybersecurity and Infrastructure Agency, Chris Krebs, publicly attested to the lack of fraud in the 2020 election, Trump summarily fired him via Twitter. Krebs's declaration stood in direct contrast to the White House's need to explain away the presidential election results as the outcome of corruption and vote rigging.

Among the most dangerous features of American Exceptionalism is the intellectually crippling idea that "it can't happen here." According to this constitutive myth, *coup d'états* are for Third World, tin-pot regimes or for the sepia-toned newsreel days of European politics before fascism was smashed by the Western Allies in the Second World War.

Such has been the prevailing political ethos that has animated so much of American political discourse for over 75 years. But Trump's approach to ruling posed serious questions for the once-prevailing liberal consensus on what makes the American political experience unique. His last-ditch, post-election tinkering with government agencies to stack the deck in his favor was, at the very least, an outgrowth and continuation of his governing style and persona. It is also consistent with the gradual consolidation of state authority that to varying degrees has subtly, if persistently, lain at the core of American presidential politics since the Nixon era. One of the curiosities of American conservatism is that it postulates a commitment to limited government but only implements it when it comes to avoiding regulation of extractive industry, finance and the environment. When it comes to security, both internal and external, a stronger government hand is required. The process of centralization is aided by the need for immediacy in decision-making as well as by surveillance technologies and data collection that enable government monitoring.

The pressures behind growing centralization of power and decision-making are complex. We have explored them in this book as part of an account of the trends that undercut democracy in America at a critical political moment. What is most relevant here is that the threat of an enhanced slide toward authoritarian power was clearly in evidence in the days immediately after the 2020 election. With the Justice Department having been securely in Trump's camp through the rule by Attorney General William Barr and with assurances of a 6–3 conservative majority on the Supreme Court in place, the normal "guard rails" preventing democracy from going off track were no longer in place. While Barr himself refused to go as far as Trump wished and denied claims of a stolen election, the outgoing attorney general had already proven himself to be Trump's water boy. That was never more evident than in the spring of 2019, when Barr completely misrepresented a redacted version of the Mueller Report on potential collusion between the Trump campaign and the Russian government. Despite substantial evidence in the document of shady, if not outright illegal, activity by Trump and his closest aides, Barr's cover letter exonerated Trump of any and all wrongdoing. Barr also refused to engage Justice Department attorneys in an investigation of right-wing terrorist violence in the United States. Yet, he continued to provide legal cover for Trump, for example through intervention to expedite a reduced penalty for disgraced former National Security Advisor Michael Flynn following his conviction for perjury—a matter ultimately voided by a presidential pardon. The attorney general's concern to intervene on behalf of Trump and place him above the law had extended even to the matter of a civil case of defamation against Trump following an alleged rape. Here the Justice Department intervened on Trump's behalf with a claim that any of his supposed defamatory statements were made in his official capacity as President and thus were not actionable. The civil court dismissed this claim, but the effort to isolate Trump from the courts was symptomatic of his refusal to submit to a legal process.

Nor was the Republican-controlled Senate positioned to fulfill its traditional function of "advise and consent" in anything but a supporting role as cheerleader for the consolidation of a centralized authority structure and a pernicious misinformation campaign aided and abetted by an army of lobbyists, think tanks, foundations and super-empowered individuals like the Koch brothers and Rupert Murdoch at Fox News. For one thing, under the management of Senate Majority Leader Mitch McConnell, the Republican majority consistently backed the president on everything from his two impeachments trials to his judicial nominees, his legislative agenda and the acceptability of storming the Capitol Building as a show of disapproval about an electoral outcome. In private, many Senators were said to find the President's mannerisms objectionable, even odious. They had even been heard assuring their Senate Democratic colleagues that their support "only goes so far" and, that if things got out of hand, they would back the restoration of civil norms rather than let the President go all out. Meanwhile, what really counts is what they actually said and did in public. With scant variation from a unified chorus of sycophants, and with only the merest murmurs of dissent on Twitter and other public media, the Republicans continued to encourage Trump and went along for the ride, later backing his cause when he was out of office and the Senate was deliberating whether to convene a January 6 fact-finding commission.

In part, these legislators supported Trump for fear of public retribution at the hands of a sitting chief executive whose vengefulness was legendary and whose political base remained mobilized. More worrisome, however, for the future of the nation's politics, these senators maintained their support (even after Trump left office), in order to appease a partisan base lest they risk facing a primary election challenge.

There has been a transactional dimension to all of this as well. With Trump, the Republican Senate was able to achieve an ultra-conservative Supreme Court for well into the next generation—something unimaginable under most previous presidents. And for all the genuflecting about budget parsimony during election season, Trump enabled Republicans to realize tax cuts benefitting the wealthy while deficit spending soared. Subsequent administrations were left with little room to implement social-welfare programs, much needed infrastructure investments or an ecologically oriented "Green New Deal" pegged to federal investment in renewable energy.

The reluctance by Congress to pursue close oversight gave the administration a free hand from the outset in such matters as nepotistic hiring practices at the White House and recurring violations of the Hatch Act, whereby overt acts of partisan campaign politicking and fund raising were undertaken by White House personnel, often using the White House to do so.

Even without an overt seizure of power, the administration and its partisan allies who questioned the election outcome did great damage to a key pillar of American democracy. The effort to bolster the loser's claims of fraud cast the integrity of the election process in a light of illegitimacy that will not easily or soon be repaired. And of course, that was precisely the intent of the fabricated concerns about election integrity—to undermine the legitimacy of standard practice and to serve as a dress rehearsal for more substantive acts in 2022 and 2024. These acts not only question the integrity of the elections but seek to reverse outcomes, by a political fiat that flies in the face of actual vote counting.

The election "loss" has already become an American version of the "Dolchstoss" legend, the "stab in the back" by which imperial Germany's military was allegedly betrayed by domestic liberals, socialists and communists at the end of the First World War. That myth played no small role in facilitating the rise of a painter named Adolf Hitler via entirely legal means in Weimar Germany to turn the country and the world upside down. It was the biggest of "the Big Lies" by which authoritarianism gains a foothold and converts wishful thinking into an assertion of will in order to make the lie come true. In the United States, that lie starts with the claim of elections somehow having been fraudulent, the process corrupted by the winner, and the outcome subject to ongoing litigation and claims of illegitimacy. By mid-2021, polls showed that upwards of half of all Republicans viewed Biden's win as an illegitimate outcome of a "rigged" process. Interestingly, they never seemed to bestow similar suspicions on the same elections that saw Republicans secure half of the Senate seats and gain nearly a dozen seats in the House of Representatives. But such is the selectivity by which a skewed view of the world operates.

All of this played out amidst an alarming rise in the infection rate of COVID-19 across the country. A week after the election was called for Biden, the new case load surpassed 200,000 a day, with upwards of 1,500 deaths daily and trending towards a near doubling of that death rate by the end of the year—a 9/11 terrorist attack per day, so to speak. In fact, that doubled daily death total (2,996) was reached by mid-December and surpassed 4,000 a day by mid-January 2021. There were no prospects slowing down the virus spread given the refusal of so many states across the American heartland to engage in minimal practices of social distancing and mandatory mask wearing. By two weeks before Christmas 2020, 300,000 had died from the virus—the same number of Americans who died in all four years of the Second World War. That number would double in the next six months. By the end of 2021 it would surpass 800,000 dead.

Communities of color were hit particularly hard by the virus and by the economic slowdown that resulted from the loss of commerce. And yet peoples of color are also disproportionately represented in the subordinate service classes required to keep things going during the pandemic—working as food preparers and deliverers, for elder-care facilities and janitorial services, and as aides and nurses in hospitals. They are on the front line of defense as well as among the most vulnerable to an airborne viral disease.

Powerful and poorly understood forces are at work in our society, forces that are the main drivers of racism, poverty and inequality. All of them are intensified and exposed in their brutal consequences by the dynamics of a pandemic. The insidious nature of transmission has made it all the more difficult for policymakers to address the issue in reasoned tones. To do so requires a commitment to the basic virtues of compassion and regard for fellow human being, virtues that are in short supply these days: a respect for scientific authority, an understanding of some fundamental truths about economy and the natural world, a sense of patience and humility about the way policy outcomes play out in uncharted futures, and most importantly a level of self-restraint and respect for others while going about one's daily life.

The partisan disagreement on health care that had nearly shipwrecked passage in 2010 of Obama's Affordable Care Act metastasized in the face of the pandemic in 2020 into Republican refusals to take seriously the full scope of the medical crisis. Fashioning a response would take a consensus on basic understandings of science, research and notions of the public good that were now unobtainable because the process became so intensely politicized. Thus, the normal stresses and strains of a post-industrial economy no longer able to serve the majority of its population have been exacerbated by a public health crisis of global proportions and with distinct national and regional responses. What was made crystal clear in the U.S. policy response since the pandemic broke out in February 2020 is that the federal government was going to take a minimal role, leaving it up to local and state authorities. This took place with the blessing of a president who all along downplayed the seriousness of the healthcare crisis, who "didn't want to alarm the public," and who continually mocked the scientific communities—the epidemiologists, the public health experts, the nurses and doctors attending to patients on a daily basis—for their efforts to slow down the infection rate.

The terrifying thing about this is the extent to which large sectors of the American public have endorsed such an approach—through their voting behavior, their refusal to wear masks, their antipathy toward vaccines, the lingering belief among many that the pandemic is a "hoax" and their reversion to a frontier, cowboy-like approach to the risks involved in infection and transmission. For the next very long while, these sentiments will continue to play out in people's refusal to get vaccinated and boosted. The entire populace pays a price for this politicization.

The vacuum at the top of U.S. authority in this regard did not begin to get resolved until Inauguration Day, 2021. Until then, the virus continued to burn across the American landscape, with states like North Dakota at full hospital occupancy while its Republican governor issued permission for COVID-infected medical personnel—doctors, nurses, aides—to continue seeing patients. Neighboring South Dakota was also a showcase for managed ignorance. With only 885,000 residents, the state lost more people to the virus by the end of December 2020 than the entire country of South Korea, population 51 million. South Dakota is one of those places where the Republican governor extolls the virtues of American-style freedom and still would have nothing to do with regulations stipulating mask wearing or vaccine mandates. South Dakota, of course, is also the state where nearly half a million motorcyclists gather north of Rapid City in August for the annual Sturgis Motorcycle Rally, producing a super-spreader event that has ravaged the state two years running.

There is a curious way in which authoritarian aspirations combine with vast areas of nascent neglect and open contempt for life. When this dynamic happens out in public, in the kind of slow-motion meltdown of democratic norms that characterizes the moral and political foundation of longstanding republics, we have to confront some serious and difficult questions. The issue here is not just the delusional, narcissistic pathology of an insecure, failed businessman. Nor can complicity with his pursuit of power be explained away as reluctance by leading legislators to offend the fragile psyche of the person at the helm of their party. We are in a whole different realm here, where social movements bubble up from extreme circumstances and create the kinds of ideological pressures and limited options by which unyielding allegiances on a mass, populist basis become activated—if not entirely excused. We therefore need to explore the ways in which countervailing forces are capable of forestalling the authoritarian temptation.

Fascism takes many forms, and it comes from many places. Those who search out its organized, brown-shirt variety replete with armbands and starry-eyed salutes might well miss how the syndrome can afflict any organized society. But its impact is acutely felt in multiethnic societies where in-group identities are consolidated and pitted against out-group identities, always by means of a skillful Cipolla, the hypnotist-magician who wielded awful mesmerizing powers over his audience in Thomas Mann's novella from 1929, *Mario and the Magician*. The fascist syndrome arises when trust in public goods is low, and doubt about the fate of public life is running high. If ever there was a society with the right admixture for this situation, it would be the United States. Steadily rising inequality has introduced whole new dynamics into the political process. The nation's democratic institutions are poorly equipped to arrest the onslaught of big monied interests and bills long left unpaid—from misguided foreign wars like Iraq and Afghanistan to reckless tax policy. Mounting social and economic pressures now infuse the political culture, and the resultant political treachery threatens to lead to widespread civil conflicts, ultimately culminating in domestic terror and war.

It would be understandable if a certain liberal tradition of American institutions dismissed the claims about impending authoritarianism as extreme and overdrawn. After all, the system seems to have held, insofar as the guard rails kept bad-faith actors in check, and Joe Biden was duly sworn in as the 46th President of the United States on January 20, 2021. To take pride and relief in such an outcome, however, completely misses how close the country came to having a national election reversed by a dissident minority. And any glib, self-serving view of the U.S. Constitution and of the tale invoking "American exceptionalism" sorely overlooks the corrosive impact of years of assault on a government and a political economy that now face exhausting its capacity to respond to the challenges of future election outcomes as well as the enhanced efforts by state legislatures to disenfranchise voters in the name of eliminating "widespread fraud."

One of the things learned by studying authoritarianism is to take people seriously for what they say. That is especially the case when what they say and do represents a frontal attack upon institutions and the basic practices of governance. That 126 Congressmen could sign onto an amicus brief on behalf of an entirely false set of claims—invented by the state of Texas in order to invalidate the election outcomes in Georgia, Michigan, Pennsylvania and Wisconsin—provides an instructive example. The Texas suit was summarily dismissed by the Supreme Court in December 2020 as not meriting a full hearing because the state lacked standing to bring the claim. It was a wholesale dismissal predicted by a virtual consensus of the entire American legal profession—with the exception of that small handful of attorneys who were brazen enough to present it. Amazingly, the House Republicans who endorsed the suit included 16 Congressmen from the four chosen states that, in effect, were claiming their own personal re-elections to be spurious. It quickly became a legitimate question of Congressional inquiry whether the act of endorsing the suit constituted sedition as defined by the 14th Amendment and merited disqualification of the amicus brief signers from serving office. But the most important points are not the technicalities about who is eligible to continue to serve; it is the meaning of this unprecedented act of mass defection from the basic norms of democratic practice.

Nor were merely rhetorical gestures involved as part of this challenge. Thus the notion that such a stance was taken for purely symbolic purposes, with the claimants knowing they would fail on the face of it and were merely assuaging the president's rage; these stances were elaborately staged, if poorly argued from a legal standpoint. Moreover, that cynical position suggests that these challenges would not have been made if supporters thought they might succeed—another absurd position. Even in the rumble-strewn aftermath of that afternoon's terrorist assault on the Capitol Building, eight Senators and 139 Representatives persisted in their claim that President-elect Biden's victory was illegitimate.

This Big Lie fervor marked the entire post-electoral season, culminating in a violent attack upon Congress itself. For two months following the November 3, 2020, election, officials at every level, from governors and attorneys general all the way to local election officers, faced partisan retribution from citizens and, in some cases, threats of physical violence against their person and family. Armed white nationalists and racist militia groups surrounded the house of the Michigan attorney general, a Democrat. The career Republican governor and attorney general of Georgia both pled for the president to denounce the threats of violence—but to no avail. When electors gathered to cast their votes as duly elected members of the Electoral College on December 14, 2020, several states had to assign them police guards for protection. Later that week, at a public gathering of the white nationalist Proud Boys in Washington, DC, intended to support Trump and his claims of a stolen election, the president helicoptered over the event in Marine One to show his assent. That night the crowd turned violent, vandalizing churches and "Black Lives Matter" signage and leaving four people stabbed and one shot.

Citizens who breathed a sigh of relief that the republic has survived threats to the basic norms of democratic governance were taking things lightly. That was the point of an important speech given on the floor of the Senate on December 11, 2020, by Connecticut's Chris Murphy. In a rare public warning of the true extent of what the country faced, Murphy spoke ominously about having to deal with a political party that had renounced electoral accountability and now refused to believe in the basic rules of citizen voting and majority rules.

> When the overthrow of democracy is beginning, and you're sitting on the sidelines, you're a collaborator. There are way too many high profile

Republicans who march around the world giving speeches about the importance of protecting democracy who are awfully silent when the attempted overthrow is happening in their own country.... It is setting a precedent, and creating conditions, that could easily overthrow the next election.

As we have tried to make clear, Murphy's warning actually just touches on the most immediate and conspicuous part of the problem the country faces. What so sorely needs to be accounted for is the dispositional context within which claims of "stolen election" resonate. The plausibility of these claims is tied to a whole series of other deeply felt resentments that animate and radicalize right-wing discourse of late in a way that has fundamentally altered the capacity of deliberative bodies to function. The same breakdown of rules of engagement in legislative bodies has also poisoned the well of so much conversation in widespread areas of civil society. Churches, family gatherings, the workplace, book groups, private clubs and friendships all have been tainted to the point where what used to be areas of disagreement and attempted engagement have now become strictly delineated boundaries beyond which it is no longer sensible to go. We have erected our own demilitarized zones (DMZs) in response, an ominous ode to the paltry virtue of citizenship in a time of anti-democracy.

We also now know that those DMZs do not suffice to fend off the organized violence that is seething among the floating army of self-styled patriots joined by more organized gangs like the Proud Boys and Boogaloo Boys, who see themselves as saviors of the country. Liberals, institutionalists and conservative critics who dismissed talk of a fascist-style military coup as overwrought and inadequately nuanced to the mechanics of American constitutionalism were roused from their naïveté on January 6. That is the day all of the White House and Congressional posturing about Biden not having been rightly elected merged with the rage outside of Washington, DC, brewing all around the country, on the Internet, among militias and in the basements of malcontents whose increasingly conspiratorial and violent views of the American polity were getting reinforcement and encouragement. Some of this had been expressed before—by the Tea Party, by QAnon, Oath Keepers, disparate armed groups resisting the Department of the Interior's Bureau of Land Management, and more recently with protests against mandatory pandemic measures like mask wearing and social distancing. We had also seen overtly violent cases of white nationalist domestic terrorism: in Oklahoma City, Charleston, El Paso and Charlottesville, and at the Tree of Life Synagogue in Pittsburgh. This time, the rage was directed en masse at those on Capitol Hill who were about to authorize the Electoral College votes. They were encouraged in their anger and in their increasingly convoluted conspiratorial assertion of a "stolen election" by men and women clad in the ordinary business attire of congressmen, senators, select right-wing media and the president himself. But this was no suit-and-tie crowd that gathered. They wrapped themselves in camouflage and tactical gear, brought weaponry in tow, and had maps delineating access into to the Capitol Building. They were ready to do battle to save Trump's presidency.

All of this with the vice president inside. The crowd, following Trump's growing ire, had already turned on the vice president, as evident in its signage declaring him a traitor and worse for having committed himself, following years of slavish devotion to every one of Trump's overbearing whims, to be more loyal to the Constitution than to increasingly crazy claims that he undo the Electoral College results. It was at precisely this moment that the march on the Capitol Building took on a qualitative shift, from a rally to a violent insurrection that bordered on a coup attempt. Senators and representatives were gathered for the solemn process of reading the results of the Electoral College affirming Joe Biden's perfectly legal election as the 46th President of the United States. Objections were expected from a group of dissident congressmen, but soon after the first of these challenges regarding Arizona had been voiced and prompted debate, the proceedings were halted when the building was breached by the mob. Within seconds Pence was swept away for his own safety, hiding from any angry mob, and likely fearing for his life and for the lives of his congressional colleagues. It must have flashed even through his mind that he was being put in a position for potential assassination by the actions and incitements of the very boss next to whom he had stood loyally for the last four years.

That is how mobsters operate. They demand loyalty. They are incapable of empathy, mutuality, respect or reciprocity. The moment it comes to saving themselves they will sell out, destroy and often even kill those who have been closest to them. What ensued was nothing like Giuliani at Four Seasons Landscaping. As historian Timothy Snyder tweeted out a week later, "The more we learn, the less this looks like a coup bound to fail, and the more it looks like plain luck that all of our legislators and our vice-president were not murdered."

It had started off as such a glorious day. Two Senate runoffs in Georgia had gone as well as possible for the Democrats thanks largely to the heroic, decade-long voter registration efforts led by former Georgia legislator and gubernatorial candidate Stacey Abrams. Her Fair Fight Action coalition led a statewide drive to mobilize the Black vote. The turnout was helped by Trump's own conspiratorial criminal incompetence (on a taped phone conversation) trying to threaten Georgia Republican officials, including the secretary of state, with prosecution if they did not "find 11,780 votes" and overturn his election day loss there. Trump inadvertently undermined his own cause on behalf of the two incumbent Republicans in the double run off, Senators Kelly Loeffler and David Perdue, by venting his frustration over his own election loss during a rambling, 90-minute talk to a bored crowd of Republican loyalists at a get-out-the-vote super-spreader event.

During Wednesday's disaster—the morning rally outside the White House and then the attack that afternoon on the Capitol Building—it had to become apparent to any observer how white the mob was. This was white rage in action. And, as it turns out, it was also white privilege in action. As they broke windows, ransacked offices, smashed doors, defiled hallways and occupied chambers, they got away with their attack without having to worry about immediate arrest or violence by the Capitol Building or Washington DC police. It was quite the contrast with the previous summer, when overwhelmingly peaceful Black Lives Matter protests against police violence were met with a massive presence of police and soldiers standing firmly in line behind shields.

The January 6 attack is a whole, long, complicated story that will take many months of investigation to unravel before we fully understand the extent of coordinated planning, collaboration with White House and congressional insiders, reliance upon police cooperation (and even the military) and whether there was a massive intelligence failure on the part of security or a refusal to operationalize properly in the face of obvious threat signaling. And then again, we might never find out if Senate Republicans continue to hide behind the shield of their refusal to honor the commission's work. One thing we can be sure of: had this been a Black Lives Matter rally, the protestors and rioters would have been met with overwhelming force the moment they approached the outside perimeter of the Capitol Building. Instead, the armed mob sauntered in, took selfies and was escorted out as if they were a junior high school chorus on tour.

All day, the imagery was overwhelming: the nation's capital being overrun by white men and women decked out in camouflage, carrying poles and flags and adorned in combat gear, some wearing tactical earpieces for communication with what may have been a central command. This was White Supremacy in action: a mob of racist anti-Semites bearing Confederate flags, swastikas, "Camp Auschwitz" signs and tee shirts signaling "Six Million Jews Were Not Enough" and knowing they had the full support of the commander-in-chief.

Contrast that with the image of a Black person (Rev. Raphael Warnock) and a Jew (Jon Ossoff) standing arm in arm, having just been elected to the Senate from the heart of the American South. Their unity that morning following their Senate wins in the Georgia run off was a powerful reminder of the alliance between the two groups during the Civil Rights Movement. The contrast with the violent, anarchist hate and rage that sought to destroy a sacred hall of law could not have been greater.

To say that we have suffered a coarsening of our political discourse in recent years also dramatically understates the seriousness of the issue we now face. We had, after all, a president who as a candidate openly denounced Mexicans "as rapists" and mocked the disability of a newspaper reporter, stalked his opponent on the stage during a debate, talked about grabbing "pussy" as a privilege he enjoys with impunity and threatened a presidential candidate with shooting—all of it dismissed by media coverage as the kind of casual talk that was explained away as "Trump being Trump." Then, as president, he tried to prevent travel immigration by Muslims because of their religion, caged immigrant children and separated them from their parents, dismissed the violence of white nationalists while denouncing peaceful protests by African Americans as riotous and was indifferent to Russian meddling in our election while dismissing with nonchalance a global pandemic or the hacking of the country's intelligence service by Russian operatives. All of this met not a murmur of admonishment by his fellow Republicans. So, it was no surprise that when his first impeachment by the House was handed over to the Senate, a Republican majority decided to hear no evidence and voted on partisan grounds to clear him without a word of testimony presented.

None of this can be accounted for simply by elected officials being "afraid" of Trump's legendary vindictiveness. True, he had reserved particular scorn for former loyalists whom he perceived to have betrayed him. The chief example in this regard would be that of the Senator who became the first attorney general in the Trump Cabinet, Jeff Sessions of Alabama. Sessions earned Trump's ire after (properly) recusing himself in the Justice Department's Russia investigation. Ultimately dishonored in Trump's eyes for this perceived act of disloyalty, Sessions was driven out of the attorney general's post and then attacked by Trump during a bid for Alabama's Senator nomination, although he had once virtually ruled the state's Republican Party. Sessions went on to lose the nomination to a former Auburn University football coach. It was one of many examples of Trump's vindictiveness being used to humiliate former allies, and no one wanted to be close to the inevitable wreckage. But such "fear" cannot fully explain away the slavish complicity of former critics like Republican senators Ted Cruz of Texas, Josh Hawley of Missouri, Lindsey Graham of South Carolina and Marco Rubio of Florida.

All too often, the assumption is that these and other congressmen go along with Trump out of fear, or because they are, in effect, being "blackmailed" in some way for hidden transgressions, and that were it not for this state of emotional entrapment they would act responsibly and stand up to Trump. Or that eventually they will come around when things get serious, and push comes to shove; until then they are merely tolerating Trump's extreme personality.

The problem with this naive suggestion is twofold. One is that Trump cannot receive such traditional, moderating advice; anyone who offered it would be banished from the Cabinet and the West Wing, even if it were to materialize. The second, and more important point here is that the notion that "adult" lawmakers could sustain for long a massive breach between their own internal values and their external demeanor is based upon a deeply flawed model of human action. It is not how people work. It is also not how the Republican Party has functioned for the past few decades. On the contrary. The deeper, sustained commitment of the Party since the 1960s—at least through the Nixon, Reagan and the Bush administrations—has precisely been in the general trajectory of a paring back of government regulation bearing on the environment, worker safety and healthcare, deregulating private banking and fossil fuel industries, a massive shift in the tax base from wealthy, high-earners to the middle and lower classes, and a retreat from the kinds of progressive globalist engagements that might include climate cooperation, immigration reform and human rights. Moreover, the entire time—though especially within the last 15 years—has seen a sustained assault on voting rights, with the emphasis upon issues of "security," what has also become code for an effort to limit access of minorities to expanded voting through gerrymandering by state legislatures, reduction in the number of polling places, demands for voter identification, pre-emptory wholesale removal of non-voters from registration lists and limits on the ability of felons who have served out their sentences to gain or regain their voting rights. All of this has been made possible by a narrowing of the scope by which the public may claim or appeal its rights and gain restitution for violations. We have seen this occur systematically in the assault on unionized workers, the dismantling of workplace safety standards and elimination of the legal recourse available to victims of arbitrary police violence, especially against peoples of color.

The point is that with or without the coarseness and the venom, the Republicans who publicly stand behind Trump do so because he gave them a unique kind of moral and psychological cover to get away with reactionary, racist and anti-progressive policies that they would never have dared to articulate to the public on their own. And yet this is who they were and are. Now they have had their chance at implementing this politics. It is the culmination, or at least continuation, of a decades-long assault on the demos—on the "public" as the fundamental entity that political power must protect and serve, with all its diversity.

For that reason, it is a terrible mistake for liberal observers and regime critics to be satisfied with having survived another electoral cycle without a military coup—though, a scenario for this, too, came up for discussion as late as the middle of December in the White House. And the question remains paramount, and not just of mere historical interest as we move beyond that very strange year of 2020: what is the opposition to do, and how are the Democrats and other political organizations best able to prepare for what has certainly been a bruising start to the Biden Administration?

Here, then, are a few considerations for standing up to authoritarianism, for resisting the dismantling of democracy and for promoting a more inclusive, political culture.

(1) Appeals to "American Exceptionalism" as a way of claiming a special status for the American regime mask the underlying violence in state building. Given the brutal history of the American founding and the first 125-plus years of its creation—destruction of native American life, slavery as the basis for an agrarian economy in over half the country, a Civil War that devastated the Southern labor force—we have no special claims in this country for having achieved some mythic "unity" on peaceable terms. Appeals to some idyllic period of the 1950s conveniently paper over the systematic racial injustice, widespread environmental despoliation, gender inequities and a general failure to prepare for a future world.

(2) Until racism is seriously confronted and repudiated as a defining element of American political culture, it will be impossible to establish legitimacy of the regime with peoples of color. Systematic discrimination against African Americans has been a staple of the country through many guises and through many apparent eras of reform. This discrimination has yet survived after slavery in the form of Jim Crow; a lynching culture; wholesale economic blockages; job discrimination; separate and unequal educational facilities; voter disenfranchisement; housing zone exclusions; predatory and exclusionary banking and loan practices; unequal access to healthcare; food deserts; criminalization of nuisance crimes and drug possession; police bias that hides behind a "blue wall of silence"; and a bail-bond system that further criminalizes poverty. Until these are addressed as fundamental matters of egalitarian principle and not simply discussed as vacuous moralizing, there will continue to be a major unbridged rift in this country that will make it virtually impossible to build basic agreement about the purpose of political pursuits in civil society.

(3) Authoritarian solutions grow in appeal the more frustrated people feel with their own lots in life. They are tempted to look for a big, quick, dramatic solution—even if it is not going to provide the outcomes they seek. But because people feel frustrated with the prevailing norms that appear to have lost their legitimacy, they grope for solutions that are borne of uniquely aesthetic appeals as a means of satisfying some frustrated yearning that has built up over a long period of time, usually by virtue of neglect of the underlying structural inequities afflicting the body politic.

(4) Inequality fundamentally contradicts the promise of American life. The stabilizing influence in any market-oriented political economy is self-improvement, of doing better and of leaving your kids and family with more than you started with—or at least of feeling as if they have the resources to do something constructive with their lives. The "what" you leave them with can vary widely—wealth, education, opportunity, health. Crucial to that generational handing down is the ability to build some kind of basic financial equity that would enable the next generation to achieve more. Yet for a growing segment of the American populace, the gap between promise and reality has never been greater. That is a direct function of the growing economic gap between the wealthiest classes and those variously described as middle class, working class and impoverished. For all of these subordinate sectors of the American economy, the gap is growing between their lot and that of the wealthy and powerful. This is a complex function—of tax law, of the growing concentration of corporate wealth, of the gap between those who work for an hourly wage and those who are salaried, or who draw their income from capital investment, or from the increasingly conspicuous cultural economy derived from celebrity status, portfolio accumulation and pay predicated on the basis of how much capital you move as opposed to how much you labor and

sweat. Until these widening gaps are closed, there will be every reason for the abandoned and peripheral classes to express their frustration in inchoate, anti-rational terms that are the petri dish culture for the spread of fascistic, violent and destructive forces.

(5) The COVID-19 pandemic has fed on, exacerbated and exposed all of the worst, most dysfunctional aspects of our increasingly fragmented civil society and the attendant limitations enshrined in federalism. The pandemic brings into sharp relief the dangers of libertarian traditions, what amounts to an every-man-for-himself ethos of American politics. Those whose toil is physical labor, who work with food, who deliver groceries and who are dependent upon showing up at work daily for their pay, have been the most vulnerable to the disease. Those who are cocooned in information processing, digital networking and the knowledge economy industries are more able to stay at home, performing work as if almost nothing has changed. The disparities in income are reflected in the disparities of susceptibility to the virus. Of course, there are also straightforward epidemiological issues that affect infection rates, with the elderly being most vulnerable. But the rates also show a predilection of those without proper extended access to healthcare and those who suffer long term chronic illnesses—exactly the kind that disproportionately afflict the poor, minorities and those in inadequate or overcrowded housing.

(6) The abject failure of the Trump Administration to take the pandemic seriously is not just attributable to the chronic sadism of the president; this failure emanated from a decision-making culture, shared by aides and many legislators on Capitol Hill, grounded in a profound skepticism of science and reason. The systematic neglect of basic research, development and rational testing is part of a culture that infested the appointed leadership of numerous regulatory agencies, including, but not limited to the Centers for Disease Control and Prevention, the Department of Homeland Security, and the Environmental Protection Administration—all of whom saw the anti-science bias cripple their ability to pursue independent research. The denial extended to the immediate circle of healthcare advisors on the pandemic, who delayed informing the public, refused to develop needed national measures for short-term protection, and propagated strategies of herd immunity rather than scientifically verified behaviors of social distancing and masking. The result has been a tragic and volatile mixture whereby weaknesses and rifts within civil society have been exacerbated by federal strategy. In other words, the pandemic was not just a healthcare crisis but was also part of a deliberate policy of studied neglect and targeted victimization, with urban dwellers, Democratic-leaning "blue" states, minorities and the elderly allowed to languish in neglect.

A parallel hypocrisy was also evident early in the "plans" to distribute the approved Pfizer and Moderna vaccines, with no national funding available, states left to their own, and inadequate infrastructure on hand to manage the distribution of the largest preventive healthcare program in the nation's history. While states were developing priority lists, there were plenty of wealthy and influential people queuing up to jump the line for the vaccine. We even saw certain select friends of the White House (including the president himself) treated for their coronavirus with specialized treatments not otherwise available to the public. As soon as the vaccine became available, Republican congressmen who had previously denounced the pandemic as exaggerated and who buffeted Trump from criticism for his handling of the pandemic were among the first in line to get themselves inoculated. One revealing example of the class politics involved is the way in which the most advanced economies of the world all but monopolized supplies of the vaccine, leaving the least developed countries without even protection for their frontline healthcare workers. This led to deadly consequences in India, where infection rates were skyrocketing in the spring of 2021 just as the numbers were going down in the United States. President Biden was able to offer half a billion doses to India out of charity, but also because demand in the United States was starting to slack off by late spring. But charity cannot be the basis of world health. A progressive politics here would see the need for widespread immunization as part of a sustained, centrally funded, globally distributed public health program that sees immunity from disease as a fundamental right and not as a commodity to be bought by the highest bidder or handed to one in need.

(7) Environmental degradation and population precarity have never been more evident as pressing concerns of the planet; nor have they ever been more cynically dismissed unilaterally, as if part of a fraudulent interest-group program involving an illegitimate agenda supposedly at odds with restoring American greatness and promoting the American dream. In fact, such efforts to delegitimize global ecological vulnerability, to hunker down instead into some kind of Fortress America posture, is a prescription for environmental disaster and a sure way to make the country more insecure and susceptible to climate change, resource depletion, desertification, intensifying hurricanes, species extinction and immigration pressures. Reinstating U.S. participation in the Paris Accords was a critical first step for the Biden Administration. But even that globalist convention has little more than symbolic significance given the limited goals for long term CO_2 reduction and meeting global warming thresholds, all without definitions of transgression, much less any sanctions for violators. Here, and with any global ecological accord, whether governing species protection, prohibition of oceanic dumping or setting limits on fossil-fuel standards for vehicles emissions, what counts is a deep national commitment to the practices of sound land management and respect for life of a diverse sort—not just the human kind.

(8) There is a curious alliance between extractive industry and deregulatory authoritarian governance, one whose mutual enablement has yet to be fully explored. Examples might readily be found in Trump's approach to mining and fracking; Brazilian president Jair Bolsonaro's policy of denuding the Amazonia rainforest as fast as possible; and the Philippine regime of Rodrigo Duterte's refusal to address issues of coastal flooding throughout the archipelago. There is, of course, nothing particularly "conservative" about the alliance between extractive industry and the state. It dates back at least to aggressive industrialization of the nineteenth century coupled with rapid anti-unionism of Fascist Italy and Nazi Germany. If the alliance does not look quite so militarized today, that is because modern managers have found more polite ways to justify the affinity, mainly basing it on a certain traditional Western view of how the world's resource base stands as an unlimited or at least unregulated resource to be used up at will for human consumption. An ecological approach to public policy that is inherently anti-authoritarian seeks, by contrast, to protect and preserve life, land and the environment in ways that demand material constraints on market economies. In this sense it becomes a matter of federal regulation and planning, working with industries to set goals and set limits within which market forces can operate. At the same time, it seeks to incentivize those technologies that might help more quickly in the achievement of those goals, whether through subsidies of innovative but initially costly technologies, bulk purchases to bring down the unit cost of cutting-edge technologies, or simple prohibitions on certain kinds of insidious practices (such as dumping toxic chemicals) or those outcomes that exceed certain carrying-capacity limits of the environment.

(9) It might sound trite, but a fundamental principle for any anti-authoritarian, progressive politics has to be a basic respect for people—including for oneself. It means treating people as whole persons, not as the embodiment of socially constructed categories like skin color, race, religion, gender, nationality or their status in a society. It means doing away with "pre-judgment," which is literally the basis of prejudice, and honoring their existence, their strengths, their limits and their emotional capacities as well as their aspirations. It means placing all of this above other, abstract constructs, like corporate wealth or stock market values. It also entails due regard for the continuity of multiple identities over extended periods of time and not just being expedient or transactional with them. It means taking engagement with them seriously, not dismissing them out of hand, or disqualifying them from having a legitimate role or vote. And finally, it means taking seriously how others judge you: having a sense of accountability for one's actions, being held to standards, being capable of shame, of guilt, of learning and of acknowledging weakness and apologizing for it.

(10) Beware of leaders who are "strongmen" without empathetic emotions or without apparent capacity for being embarrassed or shamed. They are the ones who ultimately will refuse to abide by rules and laws. They will bully their way through everyday life and political decisions alone, without a sense of limits. In a way that democratic theory seldom takes seriously, respect for persons and for self are basic to an orderly, peaceful, lawful society. Without it there are simply the acts of pure will and blind assertion.

Among the most crippling legacies of the Right's assault on democracy, equity and civility in the last few decades has been the demonization of liberalism. There is much to be said on behalf of those whose moderation in matters of policy and preservation of market economies includes basic decency, a sense of limits, a cautious approach and a sense of moral outrage at those who violate basic norms. We need more people to take up the liberal banner and to cloak themselves in a tradition that, for all its limitations as a revolutionary force, has nonetheless championed human rights, the environment, racial and gender equity, and mutual tolerance of difference and respect for basic decency.

Much the same can be said of the tradition of social democracy. Powerful elements of this tradition are well established in most Western European democracies where they have fundamentally altered the acceptable terms of political discourse when it comes to providing basic human needs and services. In the United States social democracy has only recently emerged in political discussions as a serious answer to some of the most enduring challenges of governance in free-market societies. Socialism, democratic socialism, social democracy—these have all been subject to systematic distortion and heavy-handed fear mongering. These various ideologies are deliberately mistaken for clumsy, state-centered models of centralized economic planning. But the ongoing struggle to seal off authoritarian tendencies in market societies requires careful scrutiny along several dimensions. One is the defense of basic democratic, participatory norms and rules of electoral accountability. Another is the bid to remove private money from the electoral process (despite the Supreme Court's 5–4 ruling on Citizens United in 2010). Yet another is the tack of using government regulation as a means of offsetting the most predatory aspects of a pure, unfettered market society with all of its attendant cultural supports through various guidelines dealing with the environment, worker protection, health and education services and tax policy. Without these tools there is simply too much imbalance in the distribution of collective rewards. When that balance is compromised, the polity tilts toward a centralized government that is simultaneously too cozy protecting industry and too prone to crack down on social unrest.

The tradition of social democracy thus provides a countervailing force. The complexity here is that it must do so under the umbrella of the Democratic Party. Only if that party remains large, inclusive and unusually noisy and disruptive do we have what it takes to ensure a democratic, anti-authoritarian agenda in the post-pandemic era. The real issue for our polity in the future is not that such a government would be dysfunctional. Rather, the forces of corporate and fascist partisanship simply do not want it to work at all. The only cure for this is a big, vocal and inclusive tent in which the occupants agree to keep at it for long hours. Only then can the tide of authoritarian politics be resisted and more probity and ethical decency in political life be restored.

POSTSCRIPT

Memorial Day weekend 2021 was when the masks really came off.

By late spring 2021, state by state across the United States, citizens could formally enjoy lifted restrictions on mask wearing and social distance. Those who had been vaccinated were officially allowed to dispense with social distancing guidelines. The liberalization spread even to those states like Massachusetts and Connecticut that had been among the strictest in mandating adherence. Because they also ranked among the most-highly vaccinated as a percentage of the adult population, people felt safe in opening up to indoor gatherings and in-store commerce, including restaurants and bars—though the latter were still under some modest restrictions of patron density. They joined laxer states like Florida, Texas and South Dakota that had already done away with almost all mask requirements.

Over a hundred days into the Biden Administration, the move would seem like reason to celebrate progress from the virtual shut down of the previous 15 months. It could not have come at a more celebratory national holiday. Memorial Day weekend is that traditional transition to summer-time fun, including family gatherings, outdoor engagement and sports events like the Indianapolis 500. The 150,000 spectators who gathered at the Speedway—about 40 percent of a normal crowd for the race—were drawn by the bonus offering of free vaccinations for those who wanted them. Judging by scenes of the crowd the overwhelming majority of attendees did not need them or had decided they did not want them, since virtually everyone in the stands or the infield was maskless.

In these strange times of voluntary mask compliance, expected only of those who have not been inoculated against the COVID-19 virus, we are being asked to trust individual responsibility and self-enforcement. Those manifesting a distrust of science are expected to muster the self-discipline to protect others from their decision to circumvent the easiest, most accessible passport out of infection. A very strange public choice indeed.

The lifting of social engagement rules was accompanied by another mask lifting of sorts, one that bodes ominously for the future of democracy. On the eve of the Memorial Day weekend, the Republican Party made it clear that it had nothing but disdain for an impartial fact-finding mission to investigate the January 6 Capitol Building insurrection. A Senate initiative to open up an independent investigatory commission fell short of a filibuster-proof majority. Only a handful of "renegade" Republicans crossed the aisle, all but one of the seven among those who voted for Trump's second impeachment. The majority of Republicans closed ranks at the urging of Senate Minority Leader McConnell who, in the process of harnessing support to ensure defeat of the initiative, made it clear that the core of this Republican Party is not by any means composed of scared, mindless followers of Trump but is instead in it whole heel because this, in fact, is who and what they stand for. And across the country, in the twenty state houses they control, GOP legislators were in the process of finalizing more restrictive voting regulations that would limit access to absentee ballots while politicizing control over controversial electoral outcomes. They support these positions, it seems, not out of fear of electoral retribution by a putative oligarch but because their agenda is simply one of denying inconvenient truths and suppressing the votes of minorities, thus circumventing democracy and obstructing the processes by which infrastructure is enhanced and economies equitably developed.

At a moment in the nation's history when the economy was struggling to recover from heavily restricted commerce, one of the two major political parties abandoned all pretense of a national vision for growth and expansion. Instead, and quite predictably, it reverted to a vindictive series of reactive measures intended to close down the possibility of equal citizenship and prevent the other party from contesting legitimately at the ballot box. The Republican Party also has made it abundantly clear that new faces are not welcome: that voting is considered a privilege to be monitored, allocated and restricted at will. It has also left no doubt that it reserves for itself the right to question electoral outcomes and mount campaigns, both state by state and nationwide, to overturn the results if and when it should lose.

Despite the widely documented absence of abuse in the U.S. voting process, the Republican Party has fanned the flames of disappointment into a kind of feigned moral outrage merely by raising ridiculous questions about that process. It then turns the social-media-generated discontent that it spawns into justification for full-scale review, to the point of conducting theatrical "audits" of electoral outcomes that do not follow any prescribed pathway in counting and become theaters of the absurd. By stirring up controversy and not being able to decide what, precisely, are abuses of the process, this strategy then feeds into a legislative sleight of hand whereby voting becomes subject to restrictions, monitoring and onerous burdens of registration, absentee balloting, polling hours and on-site scrutiny by self-appointed quasi-militias with nothing but a narrow, utterly cynical, partisan interest in mind. The "Big Lie" feeds the "Big Cynicism." It is nothing but a move to subvert the most elemental practice of a democratic polity.

So much of what now occupies the Republican Party and its social media networking has to do with denigration and denialism. Instead of wondering what the Biden Administration could do to address the various incarnations of the pandemic, it has downplayed the severity of the virus, attacked Dr. Anthony Fauci and other public health officials and refused to support measures that would suppress the likelihood of continued outbreaks. Instead, it deflects attention to sideshow issues like Critical Race Theory, electoral security and a retro version of masculinism.

In an era, for example, when youth are struggling to find a voice and a future, one of the two major parties decides to humiliate those on a path of gender questioning by disqualifying them from competing in varsity sports. This attack on transgender rights can have fatal consequences for those already predisposed to ideational suicide in such a precarious moment of identity formation and self-definition in their lives. And yet, governors and the leadership of state legislatures do not blanch at the thought of dehumanizing entire groups of people, denying them basic rights and telling them that their path to humanity will not be afforded in this country.

The purely negative turning away from public engagement and retreat into a besieged, reactionary identity is precisely what drives the animus evident in a host of race relations today. As if the bare economic and demographic indicators of accumulated racism were not enough to open up minds and change policy: everything from life expectancy, average family income, net wealth, high school graduation rates and employment rates. Popular street demonstrations against the ubiquity of police violence and a commitment to overwhelmingly peaceful rallies under the banner of Black Lives Matter are dismissed as affronts to public safety rather than considered part of a tradition of legitimate protest. Meanwhile, a militarized model of public policing continues to gain ground, in no small way because a considerable minority of those who staff such security forces are themselves (former) trained military. The combination of racial suspicion and heavily armed police creates a lethal, hair-trigger atmosphere in which "perceived danger" becomes an incendiary pretext for firing away at suspicious minorities. In turn, this engenders a hostile culture among the population, who end up acting like an occupied citizenry and resist cooperation with authorities. Meanwhile the Right venerates vigilantes like Kyle Rittenhouse as heros.

The toll on public trust is inestimable. The result is a tragically toxic mix of poverty, crime, mistrust and escalating violence that appears further to reinforce racialized views. If seen genealogically, as the outgrowth of prior perceptions, actions and armed practices, the situation can be defused, but only if those with their foot on the occupied population can bear to relent their pressure. In an era of increasing partisanship, ethnic schism and self-certainty, such a release valve is not likely to be found. That is especially the case if the view prevails that "both sides" are equally at fault and thus equally accountable.

This view of false equivalence in politics today only paralyzes action. It reflects a refusal to account for responsibility and makes further impasses more, not less, likely. It abandons judgment, subordinating all parties to a dilemma of impasse and obstruction that mistakes effect for cause. In the face of such a stubborn refusal to cooperate or negotiate, calls for bipartisanship ring hollow. Worse yet, unilateral pursuit of bipartisanship, such as advocated by self-proclaimed moderates like West Virginia Democratic Senator Joe Manchin, becomes a formula for a self-destructive naivete that plays into the hands of authoritarians by ensuring an impasse.

What is so interesting, of course, is that efforts to attribute accountability and to establish ownership are so quickly repudiated by those who are being held responsible—for example, the refusal to take the teachings of Critical Race Theory seriously. Instead of dealing with it or exploring its nuances, those on the defensive in the country's inevitable demographic shift seek to ban it from school curricula, thus sweeping off the table altogether the larger issues these and other critical discourses elicit. When accountability is assigned and when people or groups are held responsible, those who should bear the historical burden cry out that they are victims of a "cancel culture"—itself a euphemism for the very tasks of assigning responsibility that are key to the maintenance of a democracy.

Perhaps what the COVID-19 pandemic in all of its phases has most revealed in the United States is that, even at the risk of death, some people in positions of power are willing to abandon civic responsibility if it means being held accountable to the entire nation. The Trump Administration's refusal to address the virus seriously, and its delay in mobilizing the scientific community, revealed cynicism, contempt for the public and a refusal to consider anything other than its own narrow identity politics. The concern was to preserve the veneer of power and authority rather than to use the levers of power to address a dire public need. Reactionary nativism did not want to reveal its own vulnerability to forces outside its own immediate control. So, it denied them. Or tried to. The same cycle of cynical refusal has marked Republican politics in the face of the virus' Delta and Omicron variants as well.

This position, however irrational and counter to the public will in the face of a biomedical disaster, is the outcome of an anti-government stance that has been at the core of the Republic Party since at least the Reagan Administration. In the hands of the Trump Administration, a political ideology that openly disavowed the central government was combined with a peculiar psychological disposition to isolate itself from any scrutiny or criticism and retreat into a defensive narcissism that made constructive conversation impossible. Thus, the anti-science stance was coupled with a mistrust of a free press and an attack on the media. The core mechanisms of democratic accountability thus became devalued. Since elections are also part of that process of scrutiny, it is no surprise that the very integrity of voting is now also under attack.

Of course, the country is by no means out of the woods yet, certainly not in terms of the pandemic. The mutability of the virus makes for an elusive, constantly changing target of public policy. All the more reason to take it seriously rather than to adopt the fatalist view that it cannot be reined in—or that the difficulty in doing so automatically makes an enemy of those who would try.

Nor is this, by any means, the end of the dilemmas we have to face. The climate crisis looms large, as does a groundswell of citizen movement in the form of global population shifts and emigration trends. Nor does the government yet have the resolve, finances and infrastructure needed to address the next era of economic and technical development—the post-pandemic world, if you will. Instead, we have a country with sclerotic governing institutions and an increasingly regressive tax structure that denies the federal government the fiscal means it needs to meet its basic responsibilities and plan for the future.

In the absence of initiatives to break the current impasse, the citizenry will likely revert to more privatized means of conflict resolution as the public sphere itself slides further into authoritarianism. Hence, the appeal of fascism in a teetering democracy: to proffer a forceful solution or modicum of enforced stability when the inherent uncertainties of political practice cannot be trusted. This is the Republican temptation. It is all the party has to offer in the wake of the collapse of the postwar consensus and the widespread recognition that the American dream was largely chimerical and mainly benefited a small tranche of the populace.

There can be no doubt that people are running scared. Gun sales were up 23 percent in 2020, and for a reason; after years of declining domestic armament, 39 percent of U.S. households count as gun owners, up from 32 percent in 2016. (*New York Times*, "Pandemic Fuels Surge in U.S. Gun Sales," May 29, 2021).

That is a small piece of evidence suggesting a deeper pathology in the body politic. Trump and the Republican Party picked up on this and made it central to their platform while the Democratic Party has largely overlooked the anxiety among certain sectors of the populace. That unease will not soon go away—not when efforts to politicize it in the forms of Black Lives Matter generate even more of a militarized backlash.

There is no simple way to force an uncoiling of the dilemma that has gripped America—and that is making its way across many Western-style democracies. There is nothing easy or reassuring about prying open the levers of authoritarian reaction. The way to start is by restoring and stabilizing voting rights and by working to instill in voters a sense of the seriousness of the need to expand basic freedoms of press and elevate serious political discourse in a badly fractured social-media-dominated landscape. It also requires a commitment to a more progressive governmental role not limited to preserving private accumulation but to enhancing public investment, workers' rights, racial equity, environmental sustainability and the sanctity of a legal system that is not the private preserve of right-wing partisans.

If this book has helped open up a space where more light can now shine on these dynamics, the reality is that the pandemic exposed fault lines in the social body that are not going to go readily away. The depth of the impasse facing the country cannot be accounted for in terms of the personality of this or that authoritarian figurehead. The proclivity of popular media coverage to personalize issues or to anchor them in terms of individual figures is not a reliable guide. The spectacle of a blame-game on "who lost Afghanistan" and the accompanying attention in the fall of 2021 on the Biden Administration's immediate, short-term handling of the long-promised withdrawal reveal the superficiality of a media spectacle policy storm abstracted from history and culture.

The same could be said about discussing the efficacy of vaccinations in the face of viral mutability. In the current context it is difficult to make distinctions between, say, outright immunity and the ability of vaccinations to reduce the likelihood of getting infected and the intensity of illness. The ability to make such distinctions and, for "the other side" to hear them requires a level of nuance and openness that is sorely lacking these days.

Construction of a politics adequate to the task today requires a monumental effort. In suggesting the outlines of what it might look like, we are inspired by classical considerations of citizenship and accountability. At the same time, we are all too aware of how inadequate such an effort can seem in the face of the considerable challenges we face—as if one were merely chanting hopefully in the midst of the vortex of a category-4 hurricane. Indeed, it is precisely the increasing frequency of such "natural" events—just ask residents of New Orleans—and the growing awareness of how such storms are intensified by human-made conditions tied to climate change, that allow people to make connections beyond immediate events and to make more powerful and enduring connections as they formulate public policy. The problem, of course, is that today those acute issues that threaten to overwhelm us daily are not just climate related; they are also biomedical, as with the pandemic, as well as economic and social. And yet the temperament required of those taxed with the decision-making power to confront these issues—of pandemic, racism, religious intolerance and the exhaustion of a certain economic model—is no longer bipartisan, if it ever was. What politics must do these days is not simply formulate rational policy but reconstitute the bases of rationality and rule-governed behavior by which policy can be legislated. Those who mistakenly attribute the breakdown to both sides or as somehow the product of a deep state cabal only contribute to the further imperiling of a political culture, one that will feed directly into the hands of a violent, fascist counter movement.

The Biden Administration wasted no time in giving citizens a look at what is possible with an activist government, even if only one that has a narrow majority in the House and the slimmest of procedural majorities in the Senate. In the face of relentless opposition from Republican legislators, Biden and the Democrats were able to make considerable progress in getting COVID-19 vaccines to a majority of Americans, and pass a two-trillion-dollar pandemic relief bill. They also formulated the terms of a massive investment bill that expanded the terms of infrastructure beyond roads and bridges to include human capital, broadly conceived, in the form of education, equity, child care, environmental rectitude and broadband access. Getting it passed proved much more difficult, however.

Cabinet members and press secretaries alike made it clear to the public that their role was to provide the public with a level of clarity and a commitment to equality before the law—conditions which had not been seen in four years. Instead of ideological rigidity defined by fearful obeisance there would be lively discussion and open debate—which many traditional media pundits mistook for fractious splits rather than healthy diversity.

There still are substantial dangers—that supporters of democracy and majority rule will underestimate the degree to which the Republican Party will embrace authoritarian tactics to regain power and undermine a forward-oriented agenda. The sustained campaign in some twenty state legislatures to weaken voting rights and to install politically motivated election commissions with the power to overturn ballot results are all dangerous precedents that play into minority hands as a tactic of subverting basic democratic procedures. The most important political battles of the next two election cycles are likely to involve not just infrastructure and tax policy but the very rules of the game by which the republic conducts its elections: defining who can register to vote, with what ease, and whose ballots will ultimately count.

In the American case, a number of unique structural factors compound the difficulty of shoring up a majoritarian democracy. The Electoral College tends to favor less populated states, giving disproportionate power to conservative, rural lands over more populous, urban and minority-populated ones. Longstanding practices of gerrymandering at the state level tend to weaken the power of traditional Democratic strongholds while creating more non-competitive election grids. This makes politics more ideologically fractious and less capable of finding common legislative ground. The persistence of the Senate filibuster as a way for a minority party to blockade legislature makes it extremely difficult for parties winning a bare legislative majority to exercise their power and move their vision forward as policy. The result is legislative deadlock, a condition that plays into the hands of anti-statists and political cynics who want to prevent accommodation and progress.

The challenge throughout the pandemic is that we have seen how government can be made to work effectively and that, in some areas like public health and health insurance, there is considerable support for maintaining such an active governmental approach. Yet the political culture is so compromised that there is also ample room for sycophants to exploit a volatile media culture to popularize distortion, lies and overt misrepresentation.

The immediate task of citizenship in a post-pandemic political culture is demanding but increasingly clear. This task entails a politics of affirmative commitment, not one of denunciatory repudiation. The Democratic Party made some headway in the 2020 election cycle, but too much of it was based upon opposition to Trump and not enough of it on identifying a path forward that would include equality, environmental rectitude, and expanded opportunity—not just accelerated economic growth. With the affirmation of a vision that entails benefits and gains for the previously ignored or victimized members of the populous, the reactionary opposition can only focus simply on the costs involved and claim they are a burden not worth assuming. It is one thing to denounce police violence and argue for equal treatment. But if public clamor becomes reduced to a misleading formula of "defund the police" and does not get articulated in broader terms that address the needs of communities, of constructive policing and safer streets, then the forces of reaction will win out by default through lies and slanderous fear mongering.

The claims of citizenship entail a vigorous defense of basic democratic procedure—voting rights broadened, the rule of law applied equally, economic equity for those who have long been victimized, tax rates that reflect the ability of corporations and the wealthiest to pay, and so forth. Every effort by the government to expand rights and benefits comes at a cost, but the gains have to be repeatedly emphasized and the costs presented as needed investments that will deliver huge returns later on. Those unwilling to build a future, like those who fend off the emergence to power of whole classes of previously suppressed citizens, must be put on the defensive and denied the sway they have enjoyed for so long to establish the prevailing terms of political discourse.

The pandemic taught us that policy debates are a matter of life and death. In the wake of the January 6 insurrection, we know that democracy now faces the same fate.

Bibliography

New York Times (2021) "Pandemic Fuels Surge in U.S. Gun Sales," May 29.

INDEX

abortion rights 79
Abrams, S. 17, 112
Abramson, S. 56
accountability 18; coverage of Trump despite accountability or vetting of his views 40–41, 43–44; decline of local news and 98; disappearance of under fascism 66
Adams, H. 12
Affordable Care Act 4, 73, 80, 85, 107; Trump's lies on a new plan to replace 44
Afghan refugees 76
Albright, M. 4
alternative media spaces 49
American citizens and citizenship 24; civic virtue in age of COVID 27, 29, 38–39; disavowals of public health mitigations during COVID and 7, 29–31, 36–37, 109; endorsement of Trump/federal policies on COVID by many 108; hatred and 68–69; identity of citizenship as life-affirming *vs.* administrative burden 28; individualism and nativist discourses in vaccine politics 36–37, 109; need for deeper understanding of political/social developments necessitating new governing cultures in 71; on-line shopping trends impact on during COVID 97–98; private welfare *vs.* public welfare in 81; responsibilities and challenges of responsible media consumption and 52–56; societal costs and impacts of COVID on 89–95; Tea Party and 86; Trump's dominance of the news cycle and 40; values of social democracy for valuing political collectivity 70, 76, 85–86, 115–121; *see also* citizen participation/activism in collective causes

American conservatism: hypocrisy of limited government idea in practice of 104–105

American democracy: as "episodic democracy" 15; Civil Rights Movement (1960s) as high-water mark of 7; class as sublimated into democratic *vs.* authoritarian populism 96–97; current on life-support status of despite post-Democrats Nov. 2020 election wins 7, 109; denial of Trump's trampling of norms of in summer 2020 58; fragility of democratic norms 17–18; framers' design of protections to protect against irrationality 7; impact of geographical imbalance on political power and representation and 99–100; income inequality as threat to 77; as incompatible with late industrial capitalism 20; individualism and nativist discourses in vaccine politics 36–37, 109; journalism/media promotion of a healthy democracy *vs.* altered media landscape of Trump era 45–47; mixed history/experience of 7; need

for democratic context for rising of fascism 61–62; public sector neglect by Republicans and 4, 73–74, 114–115; requirements of for "rule of law" to flourish in 17–18; values needed for standing up to and countering rising authoritarianism and 115–121; *see also* Biden Administration; Carter Administration; democratic renewal; Obama Administration; partisan divides; Reagan Administration; social democracy; Trump Administration
American democracy during COVID 6, 8, 20–21, 28–29, 107; America in 2020s *vs.* interwar period and 77–78; civic virtue in age of COVID 27–29, 38–39; continuing political deadlock despite election of Biden 7, 79, 109; COVID relief packages and 72, 96; COVID-19 pandemic as opportunity for collective action/mobilization and 86–87, 100; current precarity of democracy 15–16, 79, 99, 109; decline of local news and 98; Democrat Senator Murphy's speech on threats to from support of "Big Lie" 110–111; disavowals of public health mitigations and 7, 29–31; disproportionate social/economic impact of on working classes 93–96, 117; effort to tame as possible template for restored faith in government 5; enclosed residences trend and 99; governors' role in compensating for lack of national COVID policy 33–34, 108; as greatest test of AND the test U.S. most ill-equipped to face 6; growing centralization of state power and decision-making 104–105; impact of on communities of color 107; immigration and customs enforcement 34; impact of geographical imbalance on political power and representation and 99–100; impacts on democratic participation 89, 99–100; income inequality as threat to 77, 90; increased privatization and 99; individualism and nativist discourses in vaccine politics 36–37, 109; masking in Presidential news briefings and/social messaging that Pandemic was not serious 31; need for commitment to compassion as value and 107; on-line shopping trends impact on 97–98; public sector neglect of Republicans and 4, 73–74, 114–115; Republican complicity in Trumps "Big Lie" as threat to 59, 103–106, 109–110; Republican's complicity in Trump's COVID mismanagement 8, 58, 96, 107–108, 114; social democracy and 70, 79; societal costs of COVID and 89–91; threat of Trump's "Big Lie" on peaceful transfer of power and 102; threats to election integrity from "Big Lie" 106–107; values needed for standing up to and countering authoritarianism 115–121; *see also* partisan divides; Trump Administration during COVID

American economy: current precarity of 15–16, 79; democracy as incompatible with late industrial capitalism of 20; Democrats' economic agenda *vs.* Republicans 73–74; destabilization of old ideas about 11; economic problems of 1970s 5; failure of economic policies of neoliberalism 74–75; hegemony of U.S. in "American Century" period and 22; lack of social safety nets in 80, 83–85; recession of 1981-1983 22; Republican Party neglect of public services and 73–74; social democracy as subordinating economy to democracy and 72, 80–82; Tax Cuts and Jobs Act of 2017 73; *see also* capitalism; income inequality

American economy during COVID 8; CARES Act and 95; Democrats 'economic agenda *vs.* Republicans 73–74, 95–96; disproportionate social and economic impact of on poor/working classes and communities of color 93–96, 107; essential workers and 16; exposure of precarious employment base in US 16, 107; impact of disregard for public health measures on 30–31; impact on rural America, Native Americans and American West of 98; pandemic relief package of 2021 and 72–73, 96; *see also* capitalism; Trump Administration during COVID

American exceptionalism 34–35, 81; danger of "It can't happen here" idea 104; need to question myth of to counter authoritarian rise in U.S. 115
American flag lapel pins 25
anti-democratic culture and politics; *see* authoritarian politics, rise of in U.S.
anti-intellectualism, in fascism 65–66

anti-Semitism, at January 6th insurrection 113
anti-vaxxers 91
Anti-Vietnam War Movement 15
Arendt, H. 12
Aristotle 10
Ashley, R. K. 12
authoritarian politics, rise of in U.S. 1–2, 9, 20, 77; America in 2020s *vs.* interwar period and 77–78; cellphone use by protestors/insurrectionists at as sign of 68; challenge of overcoming 20; Clinton Administration's moderate Left politics of endorsing Reganomics as factor in 75; complacency of American people about 7–9; contributing factors to 2; dark outcome of deeper political demonology and fascist-authoritarianism 9, 25; Democrat Senator Murphy's speech on in face of "Big Lie" and 110–111; Democratic Party leaders' failure to recognize current threats to 21; denial of Trump's authoritarian tendencies in summer 2020 57–58; election of G.W. Bush and 9/11 foreign polices as factor in 75; ending racial discrimination and myth of American exceptionalism to counter 115–116; failure/reluctance of commentators to label Trump Administration as 45, 48–49, 67, 113–116; hatred and 68–69; knowledge economies and 78; McConnell's Senate leadership during Obama as factor in 75; nativist xenophobia during Obama as factor in 75; need for mutual understanding of and adherence to democratic principles/norms to endure 19, 21; need not to dismiss despite Biden being sworn in 109; need to close income inequality gaps to counter 116–117; need to develop formidable Left-wing alternative to the Right to resist 75–76; outcome of as beginning of democratic renewal 9, 26; public sector neglect of Republicans as factor in 4, 114–115; Republican complicity in Trumps Big lie as factor in 59, 103–106; social democracy as resistance and alternate arrangement to 70–71, 79; socialism and 80; steady progression of 4; Tea Party as factor in 75, 86; threats to checks and balances by corrupt political leaders and 18; Trump's aspirations to *vs.* reality 102; Trump's stolen elections claims as clear evidence of threat of 58–59, 103–107; two outcomes of future transition from 8–9, 25–26; U.S. political history of unresolved/unquestioned national crisis as cause of 21–22; values needed for standing up to and countering 115–121; via current media culture 52–53; via firings/replacements of key appointments with Trump loyalists 103–104; via January 6th insurrection 58–59; via paramilitary crackdowns in U.S. cities (Portland and Seattle)/state-issued violence 18–19, 57; via political leaders non-adherence to democratic/constitutional norms 18; via weakened democratic institutions 17; voter suppression laws (Republicans) and 17, 79, 84, 109; *see also* American citizens and citizenship; American democracy; Big Lie campaign; democratic renewal; fascism

authoritarianism: emotional negativity of 70; intellectual antecedents and socio-economic origins of 10; lessons on from history of 18–19; Trump's courting of authoritarian leaders 57; *see also* fascism

balance of power discourses 23
Baldwin, J. 71
bandit democracy, worry over by founders 7
Barr, W. 105
Bell, D. 23
Benjamin, W. 51–52
Biden Administration 3, 68; media and social media coverage of during days following election 102; need for new political frameworks to end current ideological impasses 3; need not to dismiss authoritarianism's rise despite Biden being sworn in 109; pandemic relief package of 2021 and 72–73, 96; refusal of Trump to greet 103
Big Lie campaign 5, 44–45, 101–102; "Dolchstoss" legend as "Big Lie" of WWI and 106; conspiracy theories from 103–104, 111; Democrat Senator Murphy's speech on threats to democracy from 110–111; firings and replacements with Trump loyalists in aftermath of 2020 election 103–104; as media-driven by Trump and

supporters and 53; mediazation of the world as causing difficulties discerning truth from fiction 47–48; as move to full-fledged fascism for Trump 58–59; Republican Party polls on support for "Big Lie" by 107; Republican Senators' support for 103, 105–106; Republican's complicity in 5, 59, 103–106, 109–110, 114; threats to election integrity from 106–107; Trump's call to Georgian election officials and 112; *see also* 2020 Presidential elections; January 6th insurrection

Birx, D. 33

Black Lives Matter 14, 37, 84; masking at Trump rallies *vs.* BLM protests 37; overwhelming force against by Trump Administration 57; peaceful protests of *vs.* January 6th insurrection 113; protests police brutality of 17; protests of police brutality by 14–15, 84; protests of past as precursors to 15; *see also* racial justice

Boehlert, E. 56

Bolsonaro, J. 57

Borat Subsequent Moviefilm 102

Brennan, J. 104

Brexit 19

Burke, E. 7

Bush Administration (2000-2008) 75

capitalism 4; fascism as alternative to difficulties in delivering capitalist rewards promised to citizens in failing democracy 62–63, 65, 67, 108–109, 116; pressures of on democracy 20, 62; social democracy as subordinating economy to democracy 72, 80–82; *vs.* socialism and social democracy 70–71, 79–82; *see also* American economy

Capitol Building attack; *see* January 6th insurrection

Capitol Hill police 104

CARES Act (May 2020) 95

Carlson, T. 85

Carter Administration 22

cellphones: as diversion and obfuscation from real challenges of our time 69

checks and balances 7; threats to by corrupt political leaders 18

Child Tax Credit of American Rescue Plan 72, 85

China, rise of 5

citizen participation/activism in collective causes 3, 9, 76; counter-politics of resistance to current political situation 17–21, 82; COVID-19 pandemic as opportunity for collective action/mobilization and 86–87, 100; lessons from history of fascism 18–19; need of Left to coalesce progressive agenda of for 85; need to coalesce progressive agenda of for collective action 85; need to renew for democratic renewal 9, 19; resistance to measures blocking CRT in schools as opportunity for 84–85; social democracy and 83–85; *see also* American citizens and citizenship; Black Lives Matter; Occupy Movement of 2008-2012; social democracy

citizenship, under fascism 60; *see also* American citizens and citizenship

civic virtue in age of COVID 27, 29, 38–39

Civil Rights Movement (1960s) 15; as high-water mark of American democracy 7; voting rights and 16; Warnock and Ossoff unity as reminder of 113

civil society 62

civil unrest, growing potential for amidst instability 78

civil war 18

class consciousness in U.S. 81–82; communities of color and 107; disproportionate social/economic impact of pandemic on poor/working classes and 93–96; sublimation of into democratic *vs.* authoritarian populism 96–97

climate crisis 19, 23; *see also* environmental rectitude

Clinton Administration 74; moderate Left politics of endorsing Reganomics 75

CNN 51; Trump's attacks on 50

Cohen, S. B. 102

Cold War 22, 81; as convenient black and white narrative 22; geopolitical complexity of *vs.* simplistic narrative of in U.S. rhetoric 23

collective action; *see* citizen participation/activism in collective causes

communism 80

communities of color, impact of COVID-19 on 107

Congress 99, 106; complicity of in Trump's "Big Lie" 5, 109–110; impact of

geographical imbalance on 99; Tax Cuts and Jobs Act of 2017 73; voting rights and 16
conspiracy theories: from "Big Lie" campaign 103–104, 111; QAnon as 54, 57, 84, 111
Constitution 7, 18; Constitutional rights 76; threat of Constitutional crisis from Trump's "Big Lie" 102
corporate America: corporate seizure of politics 3–4, 75; as possible source of resistance to rising authoritarianism 21
counter-politics of resistance to Trump 18
COVID-19 pandemic 2, 94, 107; change in public lives from 11; disproportionate social/economic impact of on working classes 93–96, 117; effort to tame as possible template for restored faith in government 5; impact of on communities of color 107; impacts of on single parents 91; impacts of on the elderly 90–91; income inequality and 15, 94–96, 107; individualism and nativist discourses in vaccine politics 36–37, 109; international dynamics in 10, 90; lack of social safety nets in 80; need for commitment to compassion as value and 107; pandemic relief package Senate vote of 2021 and 72; reckoning with failure of neoliberal polices for 74; retail shopping trends during and post-COVID 97–98; signs of Left/Democrats moving away from center-to-right during 74; societal costs of 89–91; super-spreader events 108, 112; Sweden as outlier in response to 32; U.S. death rate from COVID 90, 107; uncertainty of recovery of 91; *see also* American democracy during COVID; American economy during COVID; masking; social distancing; Trump Administration during COVID; vaccination and vaccine politics
Critical Race Theory 83–84
Cruz, T. 114

de Tocqueville, A. 7
Defense Appropriations Act, refusal of Trump to mobilize 31
DeJoy, L. 17
demagoguery 60
democracy: as combination of Ancient Greek concepts of *demos* (people) and *kratia* (power) 7; critics of in pre-industrial times 7; need for democratic context for rising of fascism 61–62; need for mutual understanding of and adherence to democratic principles/norms to endure 17–19; political theorists on influence of threats of empire/authoritarianism on 29; in World War I 83; *see also* American democracy; American democracy during COVID; democratic renewal; social democracy

Democratic Party 3; economic agenda of *vs.* Republicans 73–75; failure of to recognize current threats to democracy 21; impact of Republicans' vacuous opposition to Democrats' post-Trump legislative agenda 15; need for new political frameworks to end current ideological impasses 3; signs of Left/Democrats moving away from center-to-right during pandemic 74; *see also* partisan divides

democratic renewal: climate crisis and 26; difficulty of and need for commitment to from Americans 26; effort to tame pandemic as possible template for restored faith in government 5; need to close income inequality gaps for 116–117; need to reconsider democratic culture in U.S. for 9; values needed for 115–121; *see also* citizen participation/activism in collective causes; social democracy; values needed for democratic renewal

Democratic Senators 113; failure of to recognize current threats to democracy 21; filibuster reform hold-outs 21; pandemic relief package vote of 2021 and 72; Senator Murphy's speech on threats to democracy from "Big Lie" 110–111; *see also* partisan divides

demonic politics 2
Department of Homeland Security: paramilitary crackdowns in U.S. cities (2020, Portland and Seattle) 18
Derrida, J. 9
drain the swamp 65
Dreamers 76

Eco, U. 61, 64, 67
ecological crises 20, 25–26

economy: *see* American economy; American economy during COVID
Education (Adams) 12
education and school districts: COVID-19 pandemic's impact on/school closures 89, 91, 95; Critical Race Theory and 84; post-9/11 4; school re-openings 34; Trump Administration federal approach to over states/threat to withhold funding 34
election integrity 17
Electoral College 7, 99–100
elitism charges 82
empathy: lack of commitment to as value during pandemic 107; as value in social democracy 70
Environmental Protection Agency (EPA) 20; dismantling of 20
environmental rectitude 75; as value of the Left/social democracy 72, 83
episodic democracy 15
Esper, M. 103
essential services, gun shops as 35
essential workers 16, 93; communities of color and 107
excessive history 4
extremists and extremism, January 6th insurrection and 111–112

Face in the Crowd, A 47
Facebook 46; business model of as creating information silos 49, 53–54; suspension of Trump's accounts after January 6th insurrection 46, 54
Fair Fight Action coalition 112
fake news 50
fascism: "Big Lie" as move to full-fledged fascism for Trump 58–59; "Dolchstoss" legend as "Big Lie" of WWI and 106; as alternative to difficulties in delivering capitalist rewards promised to citizens in failing democracy 62–63, 65, 67, 108–109, 116; America in 2020s *vs.* interwar period and 60–61, 77–78; cellphone use by protestors/insurrectionists at January 6th insurrection as sign of 68; constituents of 60, 63–64; as culmination of very adaptable, mobile social forces that can create dangerous instability 64–67, 108–109, 116; as deflection of self-responsibility 66; denial of Trump's tendencies toward in summer 2020 57–58; difficulty of defining/as fuzzy concept 64; Eco's fourteen defining characteristics of 67; emotional negativity of 70; as entrance of the anxious "masses" into politics 64–65, 67, 106; as escape from political deadlock in WWII and in general 77; failure/reluctance of commentators to label Trump Administration as 45, 48–49, 67, 113–115; fascist syndrome 2; hatred and 68–69; Hitler and 64–65, 67; instability of as weakness anti-fascist politics can exploit 64; intellectual antecedents and socio-economic origins of 10; irrational philosophies and mistrust of government in development of 65–67, 109; lessons from history of 18–19; loneliness and 66–68; mediazation of the world as causing difficulties discerning truth from fiction 48; middle-class frustration and 66–67; need for democratic context for rising of 61–62; need for psycho-sociological analysis of 64, 68–69; as politics as aesthetics 51–52, 116; *Reichsparteitagsglände* as fascist landmark of Nazi Germany 102; threat of in multiethnic societies 109; as uniquely late-modern dynamic 60; use of violence by 21, 58, 60–61, 64, 68, 112
Fascism (Albright) 4
Fauci, A. 33
filibuster 21, 79; Democrats on 21
Financial Times, The 74
Finchelstein, F. 58
First Amendment 55
Flynn, M. 105
foreign policy failures (Iraq) 24
fossil fuel industry 20
Four Seasons Total Landscaping 102, 112
Fox News 46, 51, 84, 105
Frankfurt School, study of fascism of 66–67
freelancing 16
Frieden, J. 20
friendship 1
Fukuyama, F. 23

G.W. Bush Administration: dismissal of science during 3
gender identity politics: gender equity as value of the Left/social democracy 83; masking refusal and 30–31

geopolitical challenges 23–24
Georgia: Senate runoff elections in January 2021 68, 96, 112; Trump's call to Georgian election officials and 112; voter registration in 17, 112; voting rights agitation in **rev** 18
Germany: "Dolchstoss" legend of WWI and 106
Gessen, M. 4, 41
Giuliani, R. 102, 112
globalization: political impasse in U.S. and 3; rise of authoritarianism in U.S. and 1
Goldberg, M. 58
governing cultures: inevitably of change in over time 10; inherent instability of 10; need for deeper understanding of for Americans 71, 82–83; need for new 3, 8, 70–71, 79
Governors, compensating for lack of national COVID policy by 33–34, 108
Graham, L. 103
grassroots movements 86
Green New Deal 106
Greenwald, G. 56
Guicciardini, F. 1
gun ownership 35

Harris, K. 72
Hatch Act 106
hatred, as allowable political dynamic in fascist syndrome 68–69
Hawley, J. 114
healthcare 16; essential workers and 16, 93–94; impact of COVID-19 on rural 98; partisan divides on as metastizing during pandemic 107–108; Trump's lies on a new plan to replace Affordable Care Act 44; U.S. as least developed of advanced democracies 35; *see also* Affordable Care Act
healthcare workers: as essential workers and 16; lack of protection of from Trump Administration on masking 31; vaccine politics and 93–94
Hitler, A. 60, 64–65, 67, 81, 102, 106

identity politics 76–77, 81, 83–84; masking and gender identity politics 30–31; mythic identity politics of MAGA America 76–77
ideological affirmation: paucity of analysis devoted to 4

ideological impasses 2–3, 14; need for new political frameworks to end 3
Ill Fares the Land (Judt) 71
immigration and customs enforcement 57; continuation of dehumanizing anti-immigration policies 79; hard line of Trump Administration during COVID 34; Muslim ban of Trump Administration 113; Trump Administration federal approach to over states 34
impeachment of Trump 5; Republican vote against 114
inclusiveness: considerations for promoting 115; as value in social democracy 70, 84–85
income inequality 73–75, 77, 106; COVID-19 pandemic as accelerator of 15, 94–96, 107; as factor in rise of authoritarian politics in U.S. 116–117
independent journalism: as value of the Left/social democracy 72, 83
India 97
individualism 36
information silos 49, 53–54
infrastructure 106; erosion of 25; post-9/11 4
insurrection of January 6th, 2021: *see* January 6th insurrection
international security debates, post-nuclear era 23; falsity of domestic hegemony model for facing 24
Iran-Contra Scandal of 1985-1987 22
Iraq War (2003) 24–25, 75
isolationism of Trump Administration 34
Italy, fascism in 60–61

January 6th insurrection 3, 5, 7, 111–112; cellphone use by protestors/insurrectionists at as sign of fascism 68; extremists and extremism and 111–112; firings/replacements of key defense appointments with Trump loyalists and 103–104; as move to full-fledged fascism by Trump 58–59; Republican Party acceptance of 105–106, 109; threats to Pence and 112; Twitter and Facebooks's suspension of Trump's accounts after 46, 54; white privilege and rage in mob at January 6th insurrection 112–113
Judis, J. 71
Judt, T. 71

Justice Department: firing of Jeff Sessions by Trump and 114; Trump's stolen election claims and 105

Kennedy, J. F. 47
Kershaw, I. 64, 67
Klein, B. 11
knowledge economies 78
Koch Brothers 105
Kolakowski, L. 68
Krebs, C. 104
Krugman, P. 58

LeBon, G. 41
Lee, B. 35
Left 2–3; citizen activism strategies for 83–84; left-wing complacency warnings 4; need for Left to recommit to working classes 86; need to coalesce progressive agenda of for collective action 85; need to develop formidable Left-wing alternative to the Right 75–76, 83–84; progressive agenda defined 79; signs of Left/Democrats moving away from center-to-right during pandemic 74; social democracy as informing 72, 84–85
legitimacy in democratic societies: promise of a better life in 16
LGBTQ-plus community, violation of rights of 57
Lincoln, A. 87
local news, decline of 79, 98
Loeffler, K. 112
loneliness, in fascist cultures 66–68
lying, of Trump 43–45; *see also* Trump and media/social media

Madison, J. 7
MAGA America 76; mythic identity politics of 76–77
mail-in ballots 17
Manchurian Candidate, The 47
Mann, T. 67, 109
Mario and the Magician (Mann) 109
Marx, K. 62
masking 38–39; cultural biases affecting Black Americans and 37; disavowals of need for 29, 107; endorsement of Trump/federal policies on COVID by many 108; gender identity politics and 30–31; individualism/self-sufficiency/nativist discourses of public identity and consequent mobilization of militarized dynamics and 36–37; levels of in U.S. *vs.* other nations 31–32; low compliance rates and impact on hospitalization and death rates 35; modeling of by international political leaders *vs.* lack of in U.S. 32, 38; politization of 35–36, 111; presumed invulnerability and refusal of 30–31; public masking of Angela Merkel *vs.* Trump's refusal 32; at Trump rallies *vs.* BLM protests 37
McConnell, M. 105; Senate leadership of during Obama as factor in rise of authoritarianism in U.S. 75
media and social media: coverage of during days following Biden-Harris victory 102; decline of local news and 79, 98; difficulty of responsible news reporting amidst misinformation/fast-paced 24/7 cable news 50–51; as diversion and obfuscation from real challenges of our time 69; failure/reluctance of commentators to label Trump Administration as fascist/authoritarian 45, 48–49, 67, 113–116; fascist aesthetics and will and 51–52; independent journalism as value of the Left/social democracy 72, 83; independent, alternative journalism as challenge to misinformation 55–56; journalistic values and integrity as defense against misinformation 48, 50, 55; lack of discussion of socialism in 80; mainstream media as best potential source for guidance in new environment of 55; media manipulation by politicians for political power 47, 51; mediazation of the world as causing difficulties discerning truth from fiction 47–49, 79; need to analyze technologies, tech giants wielding power, and impact techniques of subjectification in social media 53; niche audience marketing and 40; normalizing of Trump by 40–45, 113; parallels with authentic "aura" of original art loss concerns by Benjamin in 1930s 51–52; past media promotion of a healthy democracy *vs.* altered media landscape of Trump era 45–47; political consequences of "click bait" news analysis and consumption 46–47, 52–54; political polarization as media-driven *vs.* actual polarization hypothesis

47, 53; privacy issues in 54; proliferation of alternative media spaces 49; public mistrust of media as effect of Trump's assault on 50; reluctance to call Trump Administration fascist in summer 2020 and 57–58; responsibilities/challenges of responsible media consumption for Americans 52–56; social media business models of as creating information silos 49, 53–54; television media/cable news 50
Medicaid 80
Medicare 80
Merkel, A., public masking of *vs.* Trump's refusal 32
middle-class frustration, fascism and 66–67
military/armed service members 18; impact of Iraq and Afghanistan on 25
minimum wage 72, 96
misinformation 54, 79; difficulty of responsible new reporting amidst 50; journalistic values and integrity as defense against 48, 50, 55; mainstream media as best potential source for guidance against 55; Twitter and Facebooks's suspension of Trump's accounts after January 6th insurrection 46, 54; via social media information silos 49, 53–54; viable independent alternative journalism as challenge to 55–56
mourning, as labor 9
Mr. Deeds Goes to Town 47
Mr. Smith Goes to Washington 47
Mueller Report 105
multiethnic societies, threat of fascism in 109
Murdoch, R. 105
Murphy, C. 110–111
Muslim ban of Trump Administration 113
Mussolini 60

national anthem before sporting events 25
nationalism 10; fascism and 67; nativist xenophobia as factor in Trump election 75; use of violence for racist nationalist goals in fascism 58, 61
Native Americans, impact of COVID-19 pandemic on 98
Nelson, S. 11–12
neoliberalism 4; failure of economic policies of 74–75; signs of Left/Democrats moving away from center-to-right during pandemic 74
Neumann, F. 65
New Deal 72, 80
New York Times 27, 58; failure of to report on Trump's anti-democratic intent 45; Trump's attacks on 50
New Yorker, The 46
news, 24 hour 14–15, 50; *see also* media and social media
Nixon. R. 47
North Dakota 108
nuclear proliferation risk 23

O'Toole, F. 4
Obama Administration 4, 104; greeting of incoming President Trump by 103; McConnell's Senate leadership during as factor in rise of authoritarianism in U.S. 75; nativist xenophobia during as factor in rise of authoritarianism in U.S. 75; Tea Party and 86; *see also* Affordable Care Act
Ocasio-Cortez, A. 68, 80
Occupy Movement of 2008-2012 75, 84, 86
oil crisis of 1970s 24
On Tyranny (Snyder) 58
openness, as value in social democracy 70
Operation Warp Speed 91–92
Organization of Petroleum Exporting Countries (OPEC) 24
Ossof, J. 68, 96, 112–113

paramilitary crackdowns in U.S. cities 18, 57–58; growing potential for amidst instability 78, 111
Parler 46
partisan divides: between Americans 111; on economy 72–73; from ensuing geographical imbalances 99; on healthcare during pandemic 107–108; as media-driven *vs.* actual polarization hypothesis 47, 53; Republican and Trump efforts to create 2, 25; Republican support of stolen election claims and 106; on vaccination 86–87
Pelosi, N. 104
Pence, M. 104, 112; *see also* January 6th insurrection
Perdue, D. 112
Personal Protective Equipment (PPE) 31
Polanyi, K. 65–66, 68, 77, 82
political exhaustion of American public 5

political grief 9
political history/meaning of today's *vs.* past politics 5, 20, 76; "blame game" on foreign policy failures of Iraq and Afghanistan and 25; denial of Iran-Contra scandal and 22; foreign policy failures of Iraq and Afghanistan and 24–25; futility of looking for meaning in 8; political complexities of past resurfacing 5–6, 25–26; socialism in 79–80; Trump presidency as culmination of past unresolved crises and 7–8
political systems: inherent instability of 10
political violence 18; in fascism 68; growing potential for amidst instability 78; as possible outcome of current politics 18–19, 21, 25, 110–111; use of for racist nationalist goals as fascist 58, 61; use of violence by fascists 21, 58, 60–61, 64, 68, 112; white nationalist domestic terrorism in U.S. 111; *see also* January 6th insurrection
politically adroit liberalism model 9
Portland, paramilitary crackdowns in 18, 57–58
post-truth politics 3, 57, 79
power in political theory 9–10, 23
privacy, protection of 54
privatization: healthcare and 35; increased during COVID-19 pandemic 99; Republican agenda of 4
progressive agenda, defined 79
protectionism, shift to 19
protests Iraq War of 2003 75
protests police brutality: *see* Black Lives Matter
Proud Boys 57, 110–111
public good: divorcing of class from 81–82; need for power to be shared in democracy to secure 85–86; Tea Party and 86
public health: *see* COVID-19 pandemic; healthcare
public sector neglect, Republican agenda of 4, 73–74, 106, 114–115
public works, neoliberal divestment from 74–75
Putin, V. 57

QAnon 54, 57, 84, 111

racial justice 72, 93; need to end racial discrimination 115–116; Tea Party and 86; as value of the Left/social democracy 72, 83; *see also* Black Lives Matter
Reagan Administration 22; Clinton Administration's moderate Left politics of endorsing Reganomics 75; Iran-Contra Scandal of 1985-1987 and 22
Red-baiting 70
Reichsparteitagsglände, as fascist landmark of Nazi Germany 102
religious beliefs in U.S. 81
Republican complicity 5
Republican Party 25; acceptance of January 6th insurrection by 105–106, 109; complicity of in Trump's COVID mismanagement 8, 58, 96, 107–108, 114; complicity of in Trumps Big Lie 5, 59, 103–106, 109–110, 114; economic agenda of *vs.* Democrats 73–75; fear as inadequate explanation for support for Trump 114; impact of vacuous opposition to Democrats' post-Trump legislative agenda 15; McConnell's Senate leadership during Obama as factor in rise of authoritarianism in U.S. 75; polls on support for "Big Lie" by 107; public sector neglect agenda of 4, 73–74, 106, 114–115; skill of in creating opposition to even basic social change 21, 73–74, 84–86, 96, 106; stripping of government power by 73; vote against first impeachment of Trump 114; *see also* partisan divides
Republican Senators 112; fear of Trump as inadequate explanation for complicity of 114; pandemic relief package vote of 2021 and 72; support of many for the "Big Lie" and 103, 105–106; *see also* partisan divides
retail shopping, trends during and post-COVID 97–98
Richardson, H. C. 56
Riefenstahl, L. 102
Right: need to develop formidable Left-wing alternative to 75, 84; skill of in creating opposition to even basic social change 21, 84–86; stripping of government power by 73
right to choose, threats to 79
Road to Unfreedom, The (Snyder) 4
Rodrik, D. 20
Roosevelt, F. D. 72
rule of law 17–19

rural America: as contributor to erosion of American democracy 26; emptying out of and ensuing geographical imbalances 99; impact of COVID-19 pandemic on 98
rural areas: support for fascism and 65
Russia under Putin 18

Sanders, B. 68, 80
savings, Americans lack of 16
school re-openings 34
science, mistrust of 35–38, 65, 91; during COVID-19 pandemic 107–108; in fascism 62, 65–66; during G.W. Bush Administration 3
Selling of the President (McGinnis) 47
Senate, U.S. 18, 21; COVID relief packages and 72, 96; impact of geographical imbalance on 99; McConnell's Senate leadership during Obama as factor in rise of authoritarianism in U.S. 75; Senate runoff elections in January 2021 68, 96, 112; *see also* Democratic Senators; partisan divides; Republican Senators
senior citizens, COVID-19 pandemic and 91
September 11th, 2001 attacks 25, 75
Sessions, J. 114
slavery 115
Snyder, T. 4, 58–59, 112
social change: promise of by joining with discourses questioning power, citizenships, justice and equity voting rights 15, 17; skill of Republican Party in creating opposition to even basic 21, 84–86, 96, 106; social democracy values and collective values for 76–77, 79, 82–87; as value of the Left 72
social democracy: democratic ethos/values 70–71, 79, 87; distortion and dismissal of as "Red-baiting" 70; for informing Leftist political thinking and 72; for infusing political culture with value of our political collective/collective action for social change 76–77, 79, 82–87; need for attention of framing of political discourses of for Americans 79–80, 85; need for Left to coalesce progressive agenda 85; need to recommit to working classes and 86; question of our current damaged democracy and 72; as resistance and alternate arrangement to fascism 70–71, 79; *vs.* socialism and free-market capitalism 70–71, 79–82; as subordinating economy to democracy 72, 80–82; *see also* citizen participation/activism in collective causes
social distancing 27, 30–31; disavowals of need for 29, 107; disparities in ability to 37; for the elderly 90–91; individualism/self-sufficiency/nativist discourses of public identity and consequent mobilization of militarized dynamics and 36–37; resistance to and consequent mobilization of militarized dynamics and 36–37, 109
social media: *see* Facebook; media and social media; Twitter
social movements/emerging world powers 22–23
social safety nets, lack of in U.S. 80–81, 83–85
social security 80
social totality 66
socialism: *vs.* fascism 63; guides/resources on 71; lack of discussion/consideration of in U.S. political culture 79–82; *vs.* social democracy and free-market capitalism 70–71, 79–82; as Trumpism's shorthand for Warnock and Ossoff campaigns 68
Socialist Awakening, The (Judis) 71
South Dakota 108
Soviet Union 22, 81; failed political analysis on aftermath of dissolution of 23; *see also* Cold War
state power, growing centralization of during COVID 33–34, 104–105, 108
state-issued violence 19–20
stolen elections claims 17; *see also* Big Lie campaign
Sturgis Motorcycle Rally 108
Substack 56
Summers, L. 73
super-spreader events 108, 112
Supreme Court 18, 83, 105–106; impact of geographical imbalance on political power and representation and 100; voiding of key provisions in Voting Rights Act of 1965 16–17
Surviving Autocracy (Gessen) 4
Sweden, as outlier in response to COVID-19 pandemic 32

Tata, J. 104
Tax Cuts and Jobs Act of 2017 73, 106

Tea Party 75, 86, 111
television media/cable news 50; *see also* media and social media
Tharoor, I. 58
the end of history (Fukuyama) 23
the end of ideology (Bell) 23
TikTok 54
timidity in mainstream liberalism 22
Triumph of the Will (movie, Riefenstahl) 102
Trump Administration: comparisons to Winston Churchill after Lafayette Park deployment 4–5; courting of authoritarians by Trump 57; failure of press/commentators to report on anti-democratic intent of 45, 48–49, 57–58, 64, 67, 113–116; impeachment of Trump 5, 114; isolationism of 34; overwhelming force against Black Lives Matter protests by 57; persistence of despite excoriation and 2020 election defeat 4, 8; personal character of Trump as shaping policy outcomes 32–33, 37, 60, 104; political deviance enablers as making possible 6–8; political exhaustion of American public from 5; politics of nationalism and xenophobia of 75; reluctance to label as fascist in summer 2020 57–58, 64; Republican's complicity of in Trump's COVID mismanagement 8, 58, 96, 107–108, 114; Tax Cuts and Jobs Act of 2017 73; undoing of Obama Administrations progress by 4; view of as culmination of U.S. political history/structural factors since 1970s 7–8, 77; view of as culmination of unresolved crisis in U.S. political history of *vs.* anomaly/accident or "Black Miracle" 7–8; *see also* Big Lie campaign
Trump Administration during COVID 6; "Operation Warp Speed" of 91–92; American exceptionalism as strategy of public health policy 34–35; CARES Act and 95; contradicting of reputable epidemiologists by 33; delegitimizing national healthcare efforts by 33–34; dismissiveness of 31, 108; federal *vs.* state-level decision and policy making on/abdication of federally coordinated response to 33–34, 108; hard line of immigration policies during 34; internalization of Trump's behavior on every level of government 33; personal character of Trump as effecting masking policies 32, 37; school re-openings and 34; Trump's lie that the "virus is under control" 44; Trump's second impeachment 8; Trump's voting obstruction via U.S. post service 17; voter turnout during COVID pandemic in 2020 35; *see also* Big Lie campaign
Trump and media/social media 40; "Big Lie" campaign as media-driven by Trump and supporters and 53; denial of Trump's tendencies toward authoritarianism in summer 2020 57–58; digital disruption of Tulsa 2020 rally of 54; dynamics as domestic abuse as paralleling 42–44; failure of press to report on anti-democratic intent of 45, 48–49; intimate working relationships in media of 41–43, 58; lying of Trump 43–45; mainstream media's surprise at Trump's election 43–44; media business models creations of information silos/amplification of lies/misinformation 49, 53–54; media savviness of Trump 41–42, 50; mediazation of the world as causing difficulties discerning truth from fiction 48; nativist xenophobia as factor in 75; normalization of Trump by press/media 41–45; public mistrust of media as effect of Trump's assault on 50; reckless accusations against others by 43; self-censorship and defensiveness in media as effect of Trump's assault on 50; Trump rally livestreams 43; Trump's dominance of the news cycle and 40–41; Twitter/Facebooks's suspension of Trump's accounts after Jan. 6th 46, 54
Trump being Trump 43–44
trust erosion in government 2, 65, 77, 79; as constituent of fascism 109; mistrust along racial lines from past medical experimentation 93
truth: anti-truth in fascism 65–66; difficulty of responsible news reporting amidst misinformation/fast-paced 24/7 cable news 50–51; difficulty of vetting in today's media/social media culture 48–49, 53–54; necessity of in politics and civil society 48; post-truth politics 3, 57, 79
Twitter 46; business model of as creating information silos 49, 53–54; suspension of Trump's accounts after January 6th insurrection 46, 54; Trump on 101,

103; Trump's firing of appointees on 103–104

U.S, Postal Service: Trump's voting obstruction via U.S. postal service 17
unions: need for Left's recommitment to 86; sustained attacks on from Republicans 16, 115
upward mobility, changes in American 15–16

vaccination and vaccine politics 27, 29–30, 35, 38, 91–93; "Operation Warp Speed" of Trump Administration 91–92; anti-vaxxers and mistrust of science and 36, 91; endorsement of Trump/federal policies on COVID by many citizens 108; healthcare workers and 93–94; individualism/self-sufficiency/nativist discourses and consequent mobilization of militarized dynamics and 36–37; inequities in international distribution of 97; partisan divides on 86–87; racial bias and uneven rates of vaccination 93
values needed for democratic renewal: community, solidarity, equity, justice as needed new values 9, 75–77, 81; independent journalism as 72, 83; need for willingness to look in the mirror during Trumpism 69; social democracy for appreciating our political collective 76–77, 79, 82–87; for standing up to and countering rising authoritarianism 115–121; values created (political and social) from the dishonest U.S. past 5–6, 24–25; voting rights as 72, 83
Vietnam War 5
vitriol: as allowable political dynamic in fascist syndrome 68–70; current as worse than McCarthy era 6; over COVID 32, 37; as a structural feature of authoritarianism 19–20; in Trumpism 68

voting and voting rights 16, 83, 108; need for shoring up of 100; obstruction of in 2020 via USPS work slowdown 17; threats to election integrity from "Big Lie" 106–107; as traditional way to express discontent 16; Trump Administration allowing of state-level determination of enforcement of 34; as value of the Left/social democracy 72, 83; voter registration and rights, in Georgia 17, 19, 112; voter suppression laws (Republicans) 5, 17, 79, 84, 109, 114–115; voter turnout during COVID pandemic in 2020 35; voter turnout in U.S. *vs.* other industrial democracies 35
Voting Rights Act of 1965: Supreme Court's voiding of key provisions of in 2013 16–17, 83

war, current threat of 19, 77
warnings about American democracy 4
Warnock, R. 68, 96, 112–113
Washington Post 58, 72–73, 103; failure of to report on Trump's anti-democratic intent 45
wealth maldistribution 1; *see also* income inequality
whiteness/white supremacy 112–113; as part of fascism 62; values of whiteness 76; white nationalist domestic terrorism 111; white privilege and rage in mob at January 6th insurrection 112–113
Wolin, S. 3–4, 15, 76
working classes: communities of color as essential workers and 107; disproportionate social and economic impact of pandemic on 93–96, 117; need for Left to recommit to 86
World War I: "Dolchstoss" legend and 106
WWI 83

xenophobia 75

Zignal Labs (media watchdog) 46